Challenge
of Ice

by
Robert N. Webb

illustrations by
Arnie Kohn

WHITMAN PUBLISHING COMPANY
Racine, Wisconsin

CONTENTS

The Challenge of the Unknown

Wild winds whip and whine across the bleak arctic wasteland. Snow swirls and lashes against the jagged, razor-sharp mounds of ice, heaved up as high as seventy feet. The temperature is 60 degrees below zero.

Midnight! Yet the sun stands high in the sky, hidden by scudding clouds and blanketing snow. This is the polar region where cold, gray, frightening daylight holds sway for six months of the year. For the other half-year an even more terrifying black night covers the desolate reaches of snow and ice.

Two men fight against the howling blizzard. Their names do not matter now, nor where they come from. They are only six feet apart. But the driving snow becomes a wall between them. The first man lurches forward, hoping against desperate hope to fight his way out of this killing, white wilderness.

The second man stumbles, staggers, and falls to his knees. A raging gust of wind drives into his back, plunging him forward, downward until his body lies full-stretched and still. Minutes later only a small mound of snow marks the spot where he has fallen.

The first man leans into the wind, forcing his gaunt and pain-wracked body onward. He feels himself falling. He tries to shout to his companion for help. But his mouth is sealed. His lips are frozen one to the other. He falls. A second mound of snow forms quickly, only twenty feet from the first.

Who were these men? What were they seeking?
They were only two of scores of men who have died in the attempt to reach the North Pole. These

two, like many others before and since them, had become separated from the main exploring party and had perished. Why did they go in the first place?

Robert E. Peary, the famous explorer, described the polar pack as a "trackless, colorless chaos of broken and heaved-up ice." Sir John Ross, the British arctic explorer, had this to say: "Remember, sea ice is stone, a floating rock, an island when aground, not less solid than if it were a land of granite."

What drove such men as Peary, Ross, Roald Amundsen, Richard E. Byrd, and others to face the furies of the North—the cold, the ice, the "land of granite," in their brave, desperate attempts to reach the North Pole? What drove them in their search for a goal that had eluded man for hundreds, even thousands of years?

The answer to that question can be answered by a question: Why does man try *anything* new? He tries because of the bold challenge of the unknown. He tries, because since the dawn of civilization man has been curious. He wants to know. He *must* know. He is forever seeking to broaden his horizons, to add to the store of mankind's knowledge.

Although the important reason for most explorations has been man's thirst for knowledge, there are many others.

Primitive peoples explored in their never-ending search for food, opening up new and unknown territories. For ages, man has spread out, advanced, and populated the earth.

The true story of exploration and discovery begins with those early adventurers searching for new trade and new trade routes. Marco Polo opened up new trade in the Far East and China during his travels with his father. Christopher Columbus, seeking a western trade route to India, discovered America.

Other explorers searched the far corners of the earth to discover and claim new lands for their countries. To plant a country's flag in a new territory brought fame and wealth to the explorer and glory to his country. This was true of many who sought to be first to reach the North Pole. For many others—and more importantly—the lure was the possibility of finding a northwest passage from the Atlantic Ocean to the Pacific.

Discovery of a northwest passage was of vital trade importance. If a quick, short, safe passage could be found over the top of the world, the long dangerous trip around the tip of Cape Horn at the bottom of South America could be eliminated. Trade would quicken. European nations which sent their manufactured products to the Far East would thrive and grow wealthy.

Search for this northwest passage began four hundred years before the birth of Christ. The first known hunter for the prized passage was a Greek navigator, Pytheas. He sailed early in the fourth century B.C. from the western coast of Europe until he reached Iceland. He described the dense fog he ran into as a soft substance combining the earth, the air, and the sea. From this substance, he said, the Universe was suspended. He believed he had reached the end of the earth and turned his ship homeward.

Down through the centuries, explorers followed in the wake of Pytheas. In 1498 the Italian navigator John Cabot was commissioned by Henry VII of England to search for the northwest passage and claim for the British Crown any lands he might discover. He reached land off the eastern coast of Greenland and named it Labrador's Land. He claimed it for Great Britain but also planted the flag of his native Venice, Italy. He turned south, skirted the coasts of Nova Scotia and New England, then turned eastward off Chesapeake Bay for England. Cabot is credited with being the discoverer of the continent of North America, even though he reached the continent six years after Columbus touched the islands off the southern coast of America.

Ten years before the Pilgrims landed on Plymouth Rock, an exploration started out from Holland. In 1609, the commercial demand for a shorter, better, all-sea trade route to the Far East became even greater. A group of Dutch merchants contracted with Henry Hudson to find this route. He sailed in the small ship *Half Moon* and after many months he came upon a "great bay" leading to a "great stream." The great bay was New York Bay and the great stream was the river which bears Hudson's name.

Hudson believed this great stream would lead him through the land to the Pacific Ocean. He sailed up the great stream until he reached a point opposite the Catskill Mountains. Here the salt water became fresh and Hudson knew that his "strait" was actually a river. His hopes for a water passage through the land to China faded. He sailed on, until "the boat found it bee at an end for shipping to goe in—with but seven feet of water and unconstant soundings."

Hudson had not discovered a river across America to the Pacific Ocean, but his "great stream" led him to the discovery of fertile lands, forests, and the early heartland of America.

The first man to search for a water communication between the Atlantic and the Pacific Oceans from the Pacific side was the Englishman Captain James Cook, famed for his explorations in the South Seas. He was also the first man to explore the antarctic regions. He sailed to Latitude 71° South where a tremendous ice barrier turned him back. Two years later, in 1776—the year of the outbreak of war between England and its American Colonies—Cook was commissioned to search for a water passage from the Pacific to the Atlantic. He explored the western coast of North America. An accident forced him to stop his explorations. He sailed into Hawaii where one of his boats was stolen by the natives. Bold Captain Cook seized the king of Hawaii and held him hostage against the return of the boat. The natives refused. Hostilities broke out. Captain Cook was killed.

In later years, all attempts to find the northwest passage were centered on crossing the top of the world. During these many explorations, discovery of the North Pole became equal in importance to discovery of the passage.

Nineteenth century history is filled with the names of polar explorers. In 1850, a northwest passage was discovered by the English explorer Sir Robert McClure. His discovery was the Prince of Wales Strait, connecting the Atlantic and Pacific Oceans. However, since the strait is filled with ice the year around, it is of no value as a trade route. Not until the first decade of the twentieth century—only fifty years ago—was the North Pole actually reached.

Since these discoveries have now been made, why does man continue his explorations in the frigid, dangerous regions of the Arctic? The reasons have changed in modern times. Military establishments have been built on and under the ice near the Pole. Americans stationed there are literally on top of the world, directly between the two great hemispheres. The Arctic Ocean, for military purposes, is the most important of the oceans of the world.

Submarines prowl beneath the surface directly under the Pole. If a shorter, all-sea trade route is ever to come into practical use, it will be by means of submarine freighters which can slip under the ice and cut down the time between our ports and Europe and Asia by weeks.

Explorations still go on. The great ocean depths are practically untouched. There are still many remote regions on the planet Earth where civilized man has never set foot. These regions are being opened up every year. Parties scour the bottoms of the seas. Expeditions go forth, some sponsored by universities, some by foundations, some by private individuals.

Man will forever answer the challenge of the unknown, in space, in the deep oceans, in every corner of the earth. But the call of the wild, frozen reaches of the North and South Poles has always been the most exciting and thrilling of all the tests man has taken and passed in his eternal quest for knowledge.

The Long, Long Search

If the captain hadn't been tired . . .

If the first mate hadn't been hungry . . .

If the officer of the watch hadn't been lazy . . .

An arctic mystery stretching over more than a century might have been solved! And a noble, loving, loyal wife might have been spared years of anguish.

Turn back the calendar to the cold, gray morning of April 6, 1851. The Canadian brig *Renovation* was plowing through the icy waters off the coast of Newfoundland. The officer of the watch spotted an iceberg dead ahead. He ordered a shift in course to avoid a collision.

As the *Renovation* drew nearer the iceberg,

passing it within a few hundred feet, the officer was startled by an amazing sight. Two ships, their masts and spars broken stubs, were frozen solidly in the floating berg.

"Ahoy there, sailor," the officer called to a member of his crew. "Tell the captain we're passing an iceberg with two ships frozen in it."

"Aye, aye, sir."

The surprised sailor took a quick look before sprinting down the hatchway to the captain's cabin. He was back in minutes.

"Sir," the sailor wore a sheepish expression on his face, "sir, Cap'n says he's mighty tired. Says if there's no danger of hitting the 'berg, do what you want to about them ships."

The iceberg with its captive ships was moving slowly astern. The officer didn't know what to do. He did know that to lower a long boat and row over to the iceberg would mean a lot of work. He didn't particularly like hard work.

As he stood there unable to reach a decision, the first mate hove into sight.

"Hey, matey. Look over there." The officer of the watch pointed to the iceberg. "Those ships."

The mate squinted.

"So, there're two ships. What about it?"

"You think we ought to investigate?"

"Listen, son. This isn't any pleasure yacht. We got to make up time if we're going to arrive in Europe on schedule. Anyways, I'm going off duty and I'm hungry."

The mate strode away.

The officer of the watch raised his binoculars. He scanned the ships carefully. He spotted no signs of life. He shrugged his shoulders and turned away.

Two hours later with the iceberg miles astern, the officer was relieved of his watch. The man taking over noticed the drawn, worried expression on his companion's face.

"What's up? You look as if you've just seen a ghost."

"I have. Two of them. Couple hours ago we passed an iceberg. There were two ships frozen in it. I'm positive that those two ships were the wrecks of the *Erebus* and the *Terror!*"

"Couldn't be. They disappeared four years ago in the Arctic. Been plenty of searching parties trying to find 'em ever since. No one found any trace of them."

"Sure. I know that. I've been thinking about the whole thing. Those ships were probably caught in the ice pack. Sir John Franklin and his party had to abandon them. When the ice floe broke up—that part which held the ships—it drifted south. I just saw the *Erebus* and the *Terror*. I'm sure of it!"

"You should have investigated. Too late now."

The young officer walked away, shaking his head. He *should* have investigated. The logs of the two ships filled with important information about the lost expedition were still probably in the masters' cabins.

Had he not been lazy and unable to reach a decision, the greatest mystery in the history of arctic exploration might have been solved right then. Instead, the tragic story of a brave expedition which left England in 1845 has stretched on until modern times.

All England—all the civilized world—was at a fever pitch of excitement. Nowhere, though, did this excitement run as high as it did in the British Isles. With tremendous pride, the British Admiralty announced on May 19, 1845, that the largest, best-fitted, scientific polar expedition in history was ready to set sail to find a northwest passage from the Atlantic to the Pacific, and reach the North Pole.

This expedition was the main topic of conversation in pubs, drawing rooms, wherever people gathered. The whole nation was caught up in a patriotic frenzy.

"Good old John Bull! We'll do it!"

It is difficult in these days to understand how an entire nation could have become so excited, how its imagination could have been so fired by an expedition to reach the North Pole. Today, of course, planes fly over the Pole daily. Submarines crawl beneath it.

The only project today which raises as much excitement comes from the race between the United States and Soviet Russia to be first to land a man on the moon. Fitting the comparison more closely to the expedition of the *Erebus* and the *Terror,* supposing it were announced that two, huge spaceships were going to try a moon shot. These spaceships would carry 135 men. That was the number of men in Sir John Franklin's expedition.

The excitement would certainly run high as those two spaceships blasted off. An anxious world would eagerly, nervously await word from the adventurers.

No word. Hours stretching into days, days stretching into weeks, weeks into years. Other spaceships would race through the skies, trying to find the two which had gone before.

If those two spaceships disappeared in the universe, the situation would be exactly that of the

Erebus and the *Terror*. They stood out to sea on May 19, 1845. On July 27, two months later, at the entrance to Lancaster Sound, a few miles south of Latitude 80° North, two whaling ships spotted the expedition. The whalers watched as the *Erebus* and the *Terror* sailed away toward the horizon. A floating iceberg drifted between the whalers and the two British ships. And that was the last time anyone saw the expedition till the officer on watch on the *Renovation* spotted two ships frozen in the iceberg. They were never seen again. The iceberg must have drifted into warmer waters and melted, releasing the embedded ships to sink to the bottom of the ocean.

Two years were to pass by before anyone expressed concern for the safety of Sir John Franklin's expedition. It was expected that the expedition would stay away that long. No one worried, for no arctic exploration had been so carefully planned. The hulls of the two ships had been reinforced to withstand the heavy pressures of the ice pack and floating slabs of thick ice.

Everything for their safety had been considered.

In command was Sir John Franklin, a veteran polar explorer. Recommendation to name Sir John came from Britain's most famous arctic explorer, Sir William Edward Parry. Twenty years before Parry had led an expedition of twenty-eight men to latitude 82° 45'—the farthest point north reached for forty-eight years.

But by the spring of 1847, two years after the expedition had so bravely sailed away, people were beginning to worry. In June of that year Earl Gray, Britain's Colonial Secretary, received an upsetting letter from another experienced polar explorer, a Dr. King. He wrote:

Franklin's ships have probably come to grief and his crews have tried to make their way to the camps of the Canadian trappers, following the course of Back's Fish River, whose estuary is to the south of King William Land. Survivors must be looked for on land and along the course of that river.

Not much attention was paid to that letter. It went into the files, to be forgotten for the time being.

"My confidence is unshaken," Lady Franklin bravely stated.

As autumn storms swirled over northern waters, the whalers returned to England. The masters of these fishing craft were closely questioned. None had any report to give on the *Erebus* and the *Terror*.

By 1848 alarm for the safety of the expedition began to grow. Two ships, the *Enterprise,* commanded by James Clark Ross, and the *Investigator,* under command of Admiral Sir Francis Leopold McClintock, sailed to find Sir John and his party. They scoured Lancaster Sound. They questioned Eskimos, but they discovered nothing and returned to England. One year later, they sailed forth again. Again their search brought no results.

An aroused British public now demanded action. People talked constantly about the Arctic.

Was it possible for two ships and 135 men to vanish from the face of the earth? Prayers were said for the safety of Sir John and his men in all London churches.

Lady Franklin was a leader in attempting to calm the public's fears. "Sir John himself declared that he was in a position to hold out for five years," she announced. "It is now only July, 1850, so there is no cause at all for alarm, much less for despair."

These were brave words from this lovely lady. They were words spoken against the chill feeling she so fearfully held within.

Other expeditions were outfitted and sailed in search of the *Erebus* and the *Terror*. All failed to find any trace of the expedition.

One search expedition, commanded by Sir Robert John McClure, although failing to find Franklin, did discover the Prince of Wales Strait. This Strait connects the Atlantic and Pacific Oceans. The discovery, made in 1850, brought joy, since at long last a northwest passage had been found. But the joy was dampened by the failure of the expedition's primary mission—finding Franklin. Also, the Prince of Wales Strait, frozen the year around, was useless for shipping purposes.

England's alarm and concern for the safety of the Franklin expedition spread throughout the world. When it was announced that Lady Franklin would charter and equip a yacht at her own expense, a gallant young French naval officer, Lieutenant James René Bellot, volunteered his services.

To the French Ministry of Marine, Lieutenant Bellot wrote:

A new expedition is now being organized in Great Britain to search for Sir John Franklin. The great services of this heroic seaman are not the exclusive property of the English, and the worldwide family of seamen rightly demand a share of the honor. The French public has been deeply moved by the fate of this great captain, and the desire I am about to express to Your Excellency is undoubtedly shared by a great number of other naval officers.

I desire to be given permission to write Lady Franklin to ask her to allow me to take part in the expedition . . . and to share in its dangers.

The permission was granted, and Lieutenant Bellot sailed on the *Prince Albert* as one of its officers. The *Prince Albert* returned a year later unable to report any success. The sorrow of the British public became more acute.

Lieutenant Bellot refused to be downhearted. "I am convinced that Sir John is safe. On the strength of my confidence," he said, "I will gladly set off again in search of him, and in my heart I have a profound belief that we shall see those staunch navigators in the land of the living again."

Lieutenant Bellot did sail again in search of Sir John in the *Phoenix*. Reaching Erebus and

Terror Bay, named for the lost ships, he set out with four companions across the ice. A howling gale caused the ice to break up. Lieutenant Bellot and two companions became separated from the others and drifted away on a block of ice, never to be seen again. This brave lieutenant of the French navy gave his life in the search for the British Sir John Franklin.

In America, concern for the fate of the Franklin party ran nearly as high as it did in England. The United States Government outfitted two ships and sent them north to join the great hunt. Their search was also in vain.

In New York City a wealthy merchant, Henry Grinnel, outfitted the brig *Advance* at his own expense and dispatched her north to renew the search. Again, when the brig returned, a year and a half later, the searching party had to report complete failure.

It was now 1857. Twelve long years had passed since the *Erebus* and the *Terror* had sailed from England's shores. The first ships sent out in search of the Franklin expedition had sailed in 1848. In the nine years of search, a polar armada of thirty ships had searched the seas and the Arctic Ocean in the frozen north.

The British Admiralty admitted defeat. It struck Sir John Franklin's name from its roster of serving officers. Lady Franklin protested. The British Admiralty replied to her protest with the statement:

> To their great regret Her Majesty's Government have been forced to the conclusion that there is no further chance of saving human life. They therefore cannot see their way clear to dispatch a further expedition to the arctic seas, thus exposing the lives of further officers and men to the great risks inseparably connected with such undertakings.

This was an acknowledgment of defeat, of bitter humiliation. All England shared in it . . . with the exception of one brave and loyal wife —Lady Franklin. With the last of her fortune, she equipped the 177-ton yacht, the *Fox,* and persuaded the now retired Admiral Sir Francis Leopold McClintock to take the command. Nine years had passed since Admiral McClintock had made his first search in the barkentine *Investigator.*

Admiration for Lady Franklin was expressed publicly everywhere. In private, though, people felt that Sir Francis McClintock in the poorly equipped *Fox* had set sail on a hopeless hunt.

The anchor chain rumbled as the *Fox* hove to at Disko Island on August 11, 1857. Eskimo guides were recruited and searching parties took to the ice. A severe winter forced the searchers to return to the shelter of the *Fox.* A second search in 1858 was unsuccessful.

A year later, in February, 1859, McClintock came upon a tribe of Eskimos. Questioning took place through an interpreter. Yes, years ago, they had seen a ship caught in the ice off King William Island.

"And the men aboard?" McClintock pressed

the questioning. "Did they stay with the ship?"

The Eskimos shook their heads. "All left ship. Go away over ice."

"Which way? Which way?"

The Eskimos pointed. "Go toward Back's Fish River."

Two months later, after undergoing terrible hardships, McClintock made the first discovery as to what fate befell Sir John Franklin. In the igloo of an aged Eskimo, he came upon some

objects strange to the frozen north. He picked up a blackened spoon. He cleaned it, and as he rubbed away the dirt covering it, the monogram of John Franklin, the initials "JF," came into sight.

With more information from the Eskimo, McClintock's party set off, their hopes high. None believed there was any chance of finding Sir John, or any of his men, alive, but they felt sure they were on the brink of solving a mystery that had kept the world in fearful suspense for over eleven years.

In May, the party came upon a skeleton, still with shreds of a blue uniform enclosing it. On the clothing they found the initials F.D.V. McClintock realized that this was the body of Des Voeux, one of the officers of the *Erebus*.

Farther along, in sight of Cape Herschel, the party discovered a cairn, a mound of stones. Chilled but eager hands tore at the rocks. Inside, they discovered a tin canister which had once contained tea. Now it contained a message from Sir John Franklin himself:

> H.M. Ships *Erebus* and *Terror*
> wintered in the ice in Latitude
> 70.5 N, Longitude 98.23 W.

> May 28, 1847
> Having wintered in 1846-7 at Beechey Island
> in Latitude 77.43 28 N, Longitude
> 91.39 15 W after having ascended Welling-
> ton Channel to Latitude 77 and re-
> turned by the west side of Conwallis Island.
>   (*signed*) Sir John Franklin,
>   commanding the Expedition. All well.

The message continued in the same handwriting:

> Party consisting of 2 officers and six men
> left the ships on Monday 24th May, 1847.

This was signed "G. M. Gore, Lieutenant" and "Charles F. des Voeux, Mate."

In the margin of the note was a message written in a different hand. Looking at the writing, McClintock knew that he had come upon the solution to the mystery at long last.

H. M. Ships *Erebus* and *Terror* were deserted on the 22d April, 5 leagues N.N.W. of this cairn, having been icebound since 12th Sept. 1846. The officers and crews consisting of 105 souls under the command of Captain R.F.M. Crozier landed here in Lat. 69.37-.42, Long. 98.41 Sir John Franklin died on the 11th June 1847, and the total loss by deaths in this expedition has been to date 9 officers and 15 men.

The message was signed "J.R.M. Crozier, Captain and Senior Officer" and "James Fitzjames, Captain H.M.S. *Erebus*."

There was one more entry, below the names.

Start on tomorrow, 26th for
Back's Fish River.

The search was ended.

In September, 1859, McClintock brought the small yacht *Fox* back to England, the only ship, in all the great polar armada which had searched for years, to bring back any positive information.

In the British Admiralty, a subdued minister had the files on the *Erebus* and *Terror* brought to him. It was a sad realization that came to him as he extracted the note sent to the Admiralty by Dr. King, twelve years before. In that note, Dr. King had suggested that a search for the expedition be made along Back's Fish River. Had the suggestion been followed, many lives might have been saved.

With tired hands, the minister took out another brief note. This one was from the Officer of the Watch on the Canadian brig *Renovation*. It described seeing the *Erebus* and the *Terror* embedded in an iceberg.

The minister shook his head. It was too late now.

The mystery of the *Erebus* and the *Terror* and of Sir John Franklin and his brave men was as near solution as it ever would be. Why had the party abandoned the warmth and safety of their ships? That question is still unanswered.

As the years went by, other discoveries relating to the ill-fated expedition were made. A sledge belonging to the party was discovered in 1926. In February of 1952, Canadian airmen, forced down in a blinding snowstorm, came across another cairn containing food cached by the Franklin party.

The long, long search was ended.

Sir John Franklin is commemorated by a memorial statue in Waterloo Place in London, and by the words of a poem by Alfred Lord Tennyson, on a tomb in Westminster Abbey:

> Not here: The White North has thy bones;
>   and thou, Heroic Sailor-Soul
> Art passing on thine happier voyage now
>   Toward no Earthly Pole.

The Lady Franklin Bay Expedition

The retreat south began in high spirits. The twenty-five men sang and whistled as they prepared to move out. There were plenty of supplies. Clothing was adequate, although their footwear made of sealskin was not especially warm or comfortable. Their destination was 260 miles away. Each mile would be rugged. Each mile traveled would be filled with danger—jagged ice, smashing ice floes, high winds, snow, and storms. But they would meet the furies of the elements and beat them.

They moved out happily. Two years of arctic service were behind them. They were going home!

Eleven months and two weeks later, only seven

members of the dauntless group remained alive. Of the eighteen dead, one man had been shot on orders of the commanding officer. The other seventeen had died of starvation.

The group forming this arctic expedition was officially named "The Lady Franklin Bay Expedition." It was more popularly known as the Greely Expedition, because its commanding officer was First Lieutenant Adolphus Washington Greely.

The time was the 1880's. The United States was gripped by the same fever to be "first at the North Pole" which stirred other nations of the world in the last half of the nineteenth century. Search for a northwest passage was no longer that driving force which sent men and ships against the brutal northern wastelands. Now it was a race among the nations to be the first to reach the Pole.

The Greely Expedition had been organized under an international plan to make a scientific study of the arctic region. Nations participating in this plan were to set up one or two observation stations. A study would be made of winds, of tides, of animal and vegetable life. This early plan over eighty years ago was similar to but not as extensive as the recent International Geophysical Year.

A year of careful organization and planning had gone into the Greely Expedition. It sailed from St. John's, Newfoundland, on July 7, 1881. Two years were spent at Fort Conger on Discovery Harbor in Lady Franklin Bay and much valuable scientific information was gathered.

Several sledge parties were sent out. None of them reached the North Pole, but one of them did gain for the United States the honor of "Farthest North." It was the first time in three hundred years that this claim could be made by any nation other than England. This sledge party reached Latitude 83° 24′ North, the farthest north any man had ever gone.

Those two years of cold and hardship, danger and denial were at an end. The date was August

9, 1883. Summer was coming to an end. New ice was forming rapidly. Discovery Harbor in Lady Franklin Bay was freezing closed. The expedition could not afford to wait another day in the hopes that a relief ship would reach them.

The carefully thought-out plan had been that if the relief ship of 1882, with new supplies, did not reach the expedition, a second relief ship would sail north in 1883. If it was unable to reach Discovery Harbor, it was to wait at Cape Sabine until September fifteenth. Greely and his men would make the 260-mile trip south to Cape Sabine on foot and by small boat.

"Move out, men!" Commanding Officer Greely ordered.

Shouts of "Hooray, Hooray!" rang up to the snow-laden skies.

Lieutenant Greely was an imposing figure as he stood there in the desolate, ice-and-snow land. Strictly military, as though he were on a parade ground, Greely was in full-dress uniform. Ornate, gold-fringed epaulets adorned the shoulders of his long blue Army coat. A huge saber in its shining scabbard hung at his side.

Although he may have looked out of place in his uniform, he had a good reason for wearing it. Lieutenant Greely was a member of the Fifth Cavalry and bore a long scar on his jaw, a reminder of a Confederate bullet at the battle of Antietam. Twenty-three of the men in the Greely party were regulars in the U.S. Army, though they had long since quit wearing their uniforms. To Greely, this was a military mission and a dangerous one. He knew rigid discipline would be required in commanding men about to meet the severe rigors of the 260-mile southward retreat. The uniform was a symbol, silently demanding respect and obedience to orders.

The party left Discovery Harbor in a steam launch pulling two small boats. All three boats were heavily overweighted with men and supplies. The steam launch towing the two smaller boats looked like a fat duck with two ducklings behind her. The boats headed for a narrow passage of water between Sun Cape and Bellot Island.

Almost immediately the party was in a dangerous situation. Ice floes blocked their progress. The steam launch, *Lady Greely*, threaded between the narrowing leads until she came up against solid ice. Sun Cape was still miles away. Lieutenant Greely left the launch to reconnoiter. He spotted what he thought was open water some five hundred yards ahead. He ordered the boats pulled out of the water and dragged to the larger lead. A group of five men with axes went ahead of the human horses pulling the boats to chop down and smooth the jagged ice.

The boats, re-launched in the new-found lead, set forth again. An hour later, the lead narrowed. The men wanted to pull the boats out at once. The ice was building up pressure on all sides.

"By my order, the boats will remain in the water while I go ahead and search for another lead," Greely commanded.

While Greely was gone, the ice built up so much pressure that it popped the launch out of the narrowing lead, upsetting it and losing many valuable supplies. The men worked frantically to save the smaller boats.

Greely strode back to the scene, his beard unable to conceal the anger on his face.

"My order has been disobeyed. Who is responsible?" He glared at the group.

The men turned their heads away. There was no answer. All had acted fast. They had to. It had been the only action to take, even if it did mean disobeying a command. Many of them wondered why their commanding officer was behaving in such a strange fashion.

Incidents such as this continued for many weeks. At one time a plot was hatched to have the surgeon, Dr. Octave Pavy, declare Greely unfit to command. He would have been succeeded by the second ranking officer, Lieutenant Kislingbury. The plot failed. Lieutenant Greely continued in command.

Four days later, on the thirteenth of August, Greely, in his anxiety to move his party southward as fast as possible, nearly brought disaster to the entire expedition. They had sailed across the mouth of Carl Ritter Bay. It was still daylight at two o'clock in the morning when they came upon what looked like a tremendous mass of ice floes. It did not seem possible that the party's southward progress could continue.

Directly ahead a huge iceberg rose menacingly. It was over sixty feet high and stood there in the cold water like a sentinel ordering them to halt.

It was snowing hard. A gale roaring out of the south drove icy snow particles into the men's faces. Greely ordered the launch to steam around the 'berg and search for a passage between it and the land. Land would mean a safe place to rest.

On the eastern side of the 'berg, they discovered a split in it. When the giant iceberg had crunched aground, a mile from the shore line, it had split apart. Through this narrow chasm, Greely could see smaller ice floes with leads in them to the shore.

The passage was about one hundred yards long,

and just wide enough for the launch to slip through, her sides touching the ice. Sheer, jagged ice rose sixty feet high to form this narrow channel.

"All right," Greely ordered. "Take her through."

The men looked at their commander in amazement. Was he mad? Didn't he know the two sections of the iceberg could shift at any second? If they did, the twenty-five men and three boats would be crushed to death between jaws of ice.

"Take her through, I said." There was anger in Greely's voice. The men, drilled in rigid military discipline, obeyed. The helmsman pointed the bow of the *Lady Greely* into the narrow, frightening chasm.

Not a sound could be heard except for the puffing of the steam engine. No one spoke. Fear could be seen on every man's face. Greely stood in the bow of the boat, shoulders squared, determination showing in the tenseness of his body.

The three boats crept along the passage, bouncing from side to side against the ice. The

men looked up at the walls above them on either side. Slowly the boats moved along, fifty feet, a hundred, two hundred, two-fifty. Would they make it?

In minutes that seemed like hours, the bow of the launch poked out of the chasm into clear water. The other boats slid out behind her. Lieutenant Greely turned around as he heard gasps of fear and cries of alarm from his men.

He was just in time to see the chasm closing. The ice was coming together. The two faces of the chasm crashed together with a deafening roar. But all the boats were safely out of the death-dealing vise.

The party made it to shore that night. A welcome rest came in a protected harbor. Lieutenant Kislingbury shot a seal and the low spirits of the group were raised a bit at the prospect of fresh meat.

Food supplies were dwindling. But the problem which worried the commander most was the slow progress toward Cape Sabine. The relief ship

Proteus was due to leave in just thirty days. So far, the expedition's progress southward was no more than thirty miles. Thirty miles in six days— five miles a day. They would never make it at that rate.

Progress was slow for the next two weeks. Huge ice floes clogged the waters. Many supplies had to be jettisoned to keep the heavily loaded boats maneuverable enough to dodge the crushing blocks of ice. Lieutenant Greely ordered the men's food rations cut in half.

Dr. Pavy objected. "The men are working, fighting the ice, hauling boats almost without sleep. They must have full rations if they are to maintain their strength," he told Greely. Greely remained firm. He knew that if they didn't get to Cape Sabine before the *Proteus* departed, food to sustain the party through a long winter would be very scarce.

On the first of September Cape Sabine seemed magically nearer. The boats broke out into comparatively clear water. Progress quickened. The

navigator shot their position from the sun. They
were only fifty miles from their goal. Spirits rose.
Greely issued two ounces of rum to all the men.

A week later their high hopes were dashed
again. Near Cocked Hat Island temperatures
dropped fast. Ice began forming rapidly. The
boats had to be abandoned and sledges were built
from the timbers. The party was forced to move
from one floating floe to another by foot.

The expedition slowed to a walk. Heavily loaded sledges had to be dragged over the ice. The
men were weak and growing weaker. The sledges
were heavy. It took all twenty-five men to pull
one sledge. To gain one mile, the trip had to be
made three times.

Day dragged after day. Lieutenant Greely came
to another decision which shocked his party. "The
currents here are southward. It is my suggestion
that we land on a large floe and trust the currents
to carry us to Cape Sabine."

The group wearily and hopelessly obeyed. The
opportunity to quit the task of dragging sledges

was welcome, even though they knew the floe could break up. They could all drown in the icy waters.

A floe was found. The party made itself secure. A tent was erected. Half the party slept in it. The other half huddled in sleeping bags on the hard, cold ice.

Two days remained before the *Proteus* was due to depart. Lieutenant Greely prayed that its departure might be delayed for a few more days. But he also knew that there was little possibility of this. Winter had come and with it heavier ice. The relief ship could not risk waiting or she would be caught firm in the fast-building ice.

The floe and its twenty-five passengers moved southward. On the thirteenth of September a joyous shout came from the sentry on lookout duty. "Land! Land!" he cried.

Everyone in the party staggered to his feet and mounted an ice knoll. From this vantage point the men could see Cocked Hat Island very clearly. And just behind it, they knew, lay Cape Sabine.

Cape Sabine and the relief ship!

In the midst of their joy, the cruelest blow yet struck the expedition. A howling storm raged out of the south. The offshore winds drove the floe backward. In less than three hours the winds pushed the floe back farther than it had traveled in the last three days.

The grim realization came that all hope of reaching the *Proteus* must be abandoned. Now they must reach land, try to live through the winter until the following summer might bring another ship to their rescue.

Getting to land was a big problem. The storm had dropped, but the ice floe was far offshore, almost in the middle of Kane Sea. A gnawing fear grew in Lieutenant Greely's mind. If the ice floe drifted past Cocked Hat Island, past Cape Sabine, they would be carried into Baffin Bay and the open sea. All would perish if this happened.

The floe was swept past Cape Sabine. It was at the entrance of Baffin Bay.

The dirty weather grew worse. The ice pack

was smashed together. Floes broke up with thunderous roars. On September twenty-fifth the ice floe the party was on was jammed between two larger floes. Suddenly, it was struck by one of them with tremendous force that broke the smaller floe into two parts.

"Move! Move!" Greely shouted. "To the other floe!"

Scrambling to save provisions, the men made for the larger floe which had just struck them. The last man to leap across the widening strip of water had to be grabbed to keep him from plunging into the sea.

The group watched the floe they had just left drift away. On it was food, precious food. Gone forever.

For three more days they drifted. But the winds had shifted. Instead of being driven into Baffin Bay, they were being pushed westward. On the morning of September twenty-ninth, land was sighted. It was four miles away. This was their last chance. The party hurriedly gathered up its provisions, pitifully few by now. They made their way toward land, by leaping from one moving floe to another. At five o'clock in the afternoon the last man, Lieutenant Greely, reached shore.

The party had been trapped on ice floes for thirty-three days, shoved back and forth on Kane Sea like checkers.

All knelt in prayer.

They reached the safety of land, but it was a barren, bleak spot which Lieutenant Greely named Eskimo Point. The ironic part was that they had landed miles south of Cape Sabine where they were to have met the *Proteus*. They all knew the *Proteus* had long since departed. But what of the supplies and equipment that must have been left behind? Would they ever be able to get to them? Could the party, near the point of exhaustion, make its way back to Cape Sabine to use these much-needed supplies?

Lieutenant Greely didn't think so. He ordered two crude stone huts built to protect the expedition from a long, cruel winter. The work was hard. Driving snow and icy winds chilled the men's hands as they tore at boulders frozen in the ground to erect the huts.

Food had become so scarce that rations had been cut in two again. An even greater threat arose. Hunger, cold, despair had turned members of the party against one another. Private C. B. Henry was caught stealing food.

What was to be done? Lieutenant Greely knew it would take strong measures and a firm hand to hold the men together, to prevent them from becoming savages.

He thought back to a happier day when he visited the White House just before sailing. President Garfield had solemnly taken the young officer's hand.

"Under your leadership, Lieutenant," the President said, "I am confident that the work will be a success. The honor of our nation will be held high in this contest with other nations."

Could Lieutenant Greely possibly live up to those words of confidence?

As the Sir John Franklin Expedition of forty years before had created the long, long search, the Greely Expedition brought about the long, long rescue.

Three weeks before the Greely expedition started its southward retreat from Discovery Harbor, the young lieutenant commanding the relief party on the *Proteus* ordered the ship to weigh anchor and set a course for Lady Franklin Bay. The lieutenant was going to try to reach Discovery Harbor and rescue the Greely expedition.

The *Proteus* put in briefly at Cape Sabine. Lieutenant Ernest A. Garlington commanded the relief party. The ship was under the command of Captain Richard Pike. Captain Pike had to take his orders from the young lieutenant. When Garlington spotted lanes of water opening to the north, he commanded Captain Pike to get under way at once. The *Proteus* sailed without depositing any caches of food.

On July 22, 1883, the *Proteus* had steamed

twenty miles north of Cape Sabine when she ran into solid ice. Captain Pike tried ramming the ice. He could not dent it. The next day the ship turned back south, but the ice was closing fast. The *Proteus* was trapped. The pressure built. Toward late afternoon the hull of the vessel was crushed. The stricken ship hung suspended by the ice.

Two hours passed. The tide turned. The ice broke up with the turning tide, and the *Proteus* with all its supplies for the Greely expedition sank to the bottom. The crew escaped with sufficient provisions to get them to land and safety.

Since there was no wireless or radio communication in those days, Lieutenant Greely, desperately trying to make Cape Sabine before the *Proteus* sailed, had no way of knowing that his relief ship was at the bottom of the sea even before he set out from Discovery Harbor.

Lieutenant Garlington, his party, and the crew of the *Proteus*, made their way to the port of

Upernivik. There they were picked up by the supply ship *Yantic* and taken to St. John's, Newfoundland. Garlington immediately sent the following message to the chief signal officer of the U.S. Army in Washington, D.C.:

> St. John's, Newfoundland
> It is my painful duty to report total failure of the expedition. The *Proteus* was crushed in latitude 78.52, longitude 74.25 and sunk on the afternoon of 23rd of July.

When the War Department released this news, America was stunned. The relief mission had failed. The Greely expedition was still trapped in the North—if any of its members were still alive.

Driven into action by public protest, the Signal Office dispatched a message to Lieutenant Garlington asking what could be done, in the face of this terrible loss. What supplies had been left at the scene for Greely's party?

The reply sped back:

> No stores landed before sinking of ship. About five hundred rations, from those saved, cached at Cape Sabine; also large cache of clothing. By the time suitable vessels could be procured . . . it would be too late in season to accomplish anything.

These fateful messages were received in Washington on the thirteenth and fourteenth of September. The relief party was in Newfoundland days before Lieutenant Greely had expected it to sail from Cape Sabine.

The release of this news raised public indignation to its highest pitch. But official Washington stalled. It met these protests with a shrug and a defeated "What can we do?"

President Chester Arthur, who had succeeded Garfield, took off for Newport, Rhode Island, for a vacation at the estate of Vincent Astor.

War Secretary Robert Todd Lincoln, eldest son of President Abraham Lincoln, was indifferent to the situation. He had never displayed any enthusiasm for the Greely expedition. Now that it had apparently failed, he was ready to close the file on it.

But Mrs. Adolphus Washington Greely would not give up. "Mrs. Henrietta" fired protest after protest into Washington from her home in California. The President and his war secretary remained silent. Then Secretary Lincoln further inflamed public opinion with the cruel statement: "I do not see any use in throwing away any more money on dead men."

America was shocked.

Action came from Secretary of the Navy, William Eaton Chandler. He had long thought that the Lady Franklin Bay Expedition should be a Navy project, not one for the Army. His present enthusiasm to send out a search party for Greely was curbed by President Arthur. Chandler was told that he was not to encourage anyone to go north to look for Greely.

Mrs. Henrietta centered her attention on Secretary Chandler. Her protest and a stack of others were forwarded to the President. The wives and families of the other members of the expedition joined Mrs. Greely in her crusade.

Congress was due to reconvene in December. Since the White House and the War Department remained indifferent, the voices of protest were directed to the senators and representatives of the public.

The Congress convened. It began a long argument about what should be done and how much money should be appropriated to outfit a rescue party. Weeks passed. Recommendations were kicked back and forth between the Senate and the House of Representatives.

Should $300,000 be spent on the attempted rescue? Should it be $500,000? Or should there be no limit to the amount of money? Where could ships sturdy enough to stand the arctic waters be procured? Who should command the rescue expedition? Should it be a Navy or an Army project?

The debate droned on for weeks.

The Greely party left Eskimo Point for Cape Sabine when Sergeant David L. Brainard returned from a food-hunting exploration with hopeful words. He had found two caches of supplies on the island in Cape Sabine.

Greely knew it would be hopeless to try to bring those supplies to Eskimo Point, so he ordered the party to strike out once more for a tortuous trip to the Cape.

Footsore, their boots in shreds, the party staggered and stumbled through driving snow, over jagged ice. They reached Cape Sabine after many dreadful days. But there was no rest for the tired, sick, and hungry men. Greely ordered work started immediately on building a stone hut. They had to have shelter if they were to survive the winter. Once again, in swirling snows, high winds, and zero temperatures, the men bent their over-

taxed bodies to the numbing work. A one-room hut, twenty-five feet by eighteen feet was erected.

Despair accompanied the men as they moved into their crude, cold hut. The food supplies cached by Lieutenant Garlington were counted. There were only five hundred rations. At one ration per day per man, barely enough for survival, the party's food would be gone in twenty days. Greely cut the daily allotment of food in half.

In that cold, overcrowded hut on Cape Sabine, the first death came to the Greely party. Sergeant William S. Cross died of starvation.

The Eskimo, Jens, and Sergeant Brainard became hunters for the party. They drove their tired bodies daily in search of bear, seal, birds—anything that lived. Once they shot a bear. Another time they shot a seal, only to see it slide off the ice floe and sink into the sea.

Private Henry was caught stealing food again.

Death came for the second time in April. The other Eskimo, Fred, a true guide and hunter, died of starvation as had Sergeant Cross.

Congress finally acted after weeks and weeks of debate. The Navy was given the job of rescuing Greely and his men. Commander Winfield Scott Schley was named to head the rescue attempt. Ships were procured from Great Britain. England had become as interested in Greely's rescue as America had been in the search for Sir John Franklin forty years before.

The rescue ships *Bear* and *Thetis* sailed from New York and Newfoundland in April and May. They steamed north under forced draft, their boilers near the point of exploding.

Reaching Baffin Bay, the rescue became a race between the Navy ships and two whaling ships. A reward of $25,000 was put up for the rescue of Greely. The whalers abandoned their fishing to try for the reward.

On Cape Sabine in April, the month the *Bear* left Newfoundland, the food supplies for the remaining twenty-three members of the expedition were down to five pounds of meat, three pounds of bread, and two pounds of stearine, the cooking fuel.

Death now struck almost daily. Dr. Pavy, Lieutenant Kislingbury, and several enlisted men died. Lieutenant James B. Lockwood, a member of the party which had gone "Farthest North," died. Starvation ruled the camp. Dishonor moved in.

Private Henry was caught stealing food again. He confessed his theft to Lieutenant Greely and promised not to do it again. Two days later, he broke his promise. Lieutenant Greely was forced to take drastic action. He ordered Sergeants Brainard, Long, and Frederick to shoot Henry.

Lieutenant Greely took three guns. He loaded cartridges in two of the guns and a blank in the third. This way, none of the three men would ever know who fired the shot that killed their thieving comrade. Once outside the stone hut, the three held a conference.

"Ammunition is scarce," Sergeant Brainard

said meaningfully. The men stared at each other.

"We're down to our last box of shells," Sergeant Long replied. "We need every shell we have for hunting."

The three were silent for a minute. Then they inspected their rifles. The blank shell and one cartridge were removed. They would use only one shell in killing their comrade. They took a solemn oath. None of them would ever reveal who actually shot Private Henry.

Private Henry, guessing his fate, had fled.

The manhunt began. Ten minutes later a single shot rang out over the snow-covered island. Private Henry would steal no more.

A few days later, on the fifteenth of May, all food was gone.

Only seven members of the party were alive.

Sergeant Brainard managed to catch a few shrimps each day. On these tiny sea morsels the seven had to survive.

One month later, the *Bear* and the *Thetis* cracked through the ice barrier off Cape York and plowed into open water in the Kane Sea. The whalers were unable to force passage through the thick ice and they abandoned their search.

The *Bear* and the *Thetis* scoured the sea. Commander Schley, in the crow's nest, the lookout post atop the tallest mast, remained on duty twenty hours a day. His stern vigil fired the crews of both ships to extreme efforts. Landings were made frequently.

In the stone hut on Cape Sabine, Greely and the six others lay silent. No word had been spoken for hours. Talking required too much effort. It was the twenty-third of June. The waters around Cape Sabine were free of ice. Finally, with great effort, Greely spoke.

"Sergeant Brainard, I wonder if you and Sergeant Long have strength to go out and look for a ship?"

The two men answered with nods of their heads. They crawled out of the hut, staggered to their feet, and slowly moved across the island to the shore of the Kane Sea.

They stood scanning the waters. At first they could not believe their eyes. They grabbed one another's arms. They were looking at the *Thetis*. They waved their arms. They tried to shout. Then, they saw a signal from the ship. They had been spotted. They were saved.

Commander Schley landed a rescue party in a long boat thirty minutes later. The surgeon gave the survivors a small amount of food. They cried for more. It was refused. The surgeon knew that too much food, too soon, could kill the starved survivors.

"Greely, is this you?" Schley asked.

In a feeble whisper Greely replied, "Yes . . . seven of us left . . . here we are . . . dying like men. Did what I came to do . . . beat the record."

Two hours later the seven survivors were carried on stretchers to the *Thetis*. The life-saving boat turned south. One more member of the Greely Expedition died on the return trip.

Twenty-five brave and gallant men had gone into the frozen north. Six returned.

On Top
of the World

A howling, driving, piercing gale swept across the frozen arctic wasteland. The temperature was fifty degrees below zero. Bitter wind and biting cold had burned the man's face until the skin was cracked.

The goal was within reach, almost within sight. Only thirty-five miles remained between this man and a pinpoint marking the top of the world. The pinpoint was Latitude 90° North—the North Pole.

Would he make it? Would this centuries-old dream of man become a reality? Would he succeed where scores of others had failed?

Commander Robert E. Peary held up his

mittened hand with its palm toward the Pole. With a sweeping, downward motion, he shouted, "Onward!"

"Mush! Mush!" responded the sledge drivers—and the final dash was on!

Only thirty-five miles to go! But thirty-five treacherous miles where every step could mean the end. Death could come in a split second. The ice beneath the party's tired feet could crack wide open at any moment, plunging the commander and his weary, loyal men into the icy bath of death.

It was midnight, April 5, 1909. The sun high in the sky. This was the period of continuous daylight. Twelve hours would tell a tale of success or failure. The commander was determined to reach his goal by noon of the sixth of April.

Six times before, Commander Peary had driven against the Arctic in attempts to reach the North Pole. Six times he had been hurled back by raging storms, crunching ice floes, hunger and sickness. Now, for the seventh time he was risking his life, and the lives of others, to gain a goal that had defied man for hundreds of years.

He knew this must be his last attempt. Commander Peary was fifty-three years old. He was still strong, alert, still driven by an unbending spirit and desire to attain his lifetime ambition. But arctic explorations demand a lot of a man and take much from him. At his age, Commander Peary knew he must give every bit of his strength, his determination, his experience in this final attempt. There could be no more.

"This was the time," he wrote, "for which I had reserved all my energies, the time for which I had worked for twenty-two years, for which I had lived the simple life and trained myself as for a race."

Robert E. Peary was first seized with "arctic fever" when he was twenty-nine years old. In 1885 he read accounts of the explorations into Greenland by the Swedish explorer Nordenskjöl. The descriptions fired Peary's imagination. The following summer he went to Greenland. His dream of being the first man to reach the North Pole began.

Years were to pass before a Peary North Pole expedition was organized and actually put into operation. The first one went north to try to reach the Pole in 1898. It was unsuccessful. So were the next five. Peary did, though, regain for the United States the honor for the record of "farthest north." On one expedition he reached latitude 83° 52′. In another trip his party touched 84° 17′. On his sixth trip, in 1905-06, he went farther north than any man in history, reaching 87° 6′. He had broken the record set by an Italian explorer, the Duke of Abruzzi, in 1900.

The sixth Peary expedition, which reached 87° 6′, was a bitter disappointment for the commander. With one degree of latitude equal to about sixty-nine miles, he was less than two hundred miles from his goal, when "leads," open water in the ice surrounding the Pole, forced him to turn back. On this attempt he nearly died of starvation making his return trip to the mainland.

His toes were frozen off, and he was forced to eat the dogs of his sledge team to remain alive.

Even though Peary failed to reach the Pole on his sixth expedition, his feat of going farther north than any other man in history was hailed throughout the world. The imagination of the people of the United States was fired with arctic fever. People wanted him to realize his dream. President Theodore Roosevelt praised Peary's attempts. Money was raised immediately, and plans began taking shape for a seventh assault on the Pole. The polar ship *Roosevelt* which had carried Peary's party north in 1905 was refitted.

There were many disappointments before the *Roosevelt* was finally ready to sail. Two years dragged by until in 1908 Commander Peary gave the order, "Cast off!" and the *Roosevelt* sailed from a pier on the East River in New York City, and pointed her bow northward.

In the months before the *Roosevelt* sailed, Peary's mail box was stuffed every day with suggestions from people who were with him in spirit.

Some made sense; most were nonsense. Some urged him to use a "flying machine," because the Wright brothers had made their first successful flight only five years before. The suggesters had the right idea too soon. Today, of course, planes fly over the Pole almost daily.

Someone else suggested that Peary use a submarine. Peary put this suggestion aside with a wry remark. "My correspondent felt sure this would do the trick, though he did not explain how we were to get *up* through the rough ice after we had traveled to the Pole beneath it." Over fifty years later, in 1959, the atomic-powered submarine *Skate* did come up through the ice at the Pole.

Other suggestions were really funny. One letter advised the commander to set up a portable sawmill on the shore of the polar sea. Lumber would be shaped for building a wooden tunnel over the sea ice, all the way to the Pole, a distance of several hundred miles.

Still another well-wisher wanted Peary to set

up a soup kitchen along the same shore where the sawmill suggester wanted the mill placed. Said the soup-lover, "Pipe hot soup through a series of hose lines stretching from the shore to the Pole." He suggested a faucet every so many miles where the party could drain hot soup into their bowls, thus eliminating the necessity of carrying food supplies. Just how that soup was to remain unfrozen in temperatures averaging fifty degrees below zero, the soup-suggester failed to explain.

"The gem of all these suggestions," Commander Peary wrote, "came from an 'inventor' who wanted me to play the part of a 'human cannonball.'" The cannon was to be aimed at the Pole from the edge of the polar sea. Peary was to climb into the cannon and hold on to the cannon ball. Bang! All Peary had to do was hold on long enough "and it would shoot me to the Pole without fail.

"This was surely a man of one idea," continued Peary. "He was so intent on getting me shot to the Pole that he seemed to be utterly careless of what happened to me in the process of landing there or how I should get back."

The suggestions were imaginative or comical but, needless to say, not at all practical. Commander Peary stuck with a tried and true method of transportation, a boat.

The *Roosevelt's* sailing was a gay affair. It left its East River pier for the coldest spot on earth on the hottest day New York had had for many years. Thirteen deaths from heat and seventy-two heat prostrations took place in New York that day.

Factory whistles screamed "good-bye" and "good luck" to the *Roosevelt* as it steamed up the East River toward Long Island Sound, and tugboats and ocean liners sounded salutes. The date of sailing from New York was July 6, 1908. An anxious, interested world was to wait fifteen months before it learned whether the commander and his band of brave and daring men had reached their goal.

The sturdy *Roosevelt* steamed up the eastern

coast of North America, her first stop Sydney, on Cape Breton in Nova Scotia. Here she refueled, her decks piled high with coal. From Sydney, the jumping-off place for the Arctic Circle, her course took her through Belle Island Strait into Davis Strait which separates Northern Canada and Greenland.

Ever northward steamed the *Roosevelt,* through Davis Strait, brushing against icebergs as she entered Baffin Bay. From Baffin Bay the sturdy steamer had to pass through Smith Sound, then into Kane Basin. Leaving Kane Basin, the *Roosevelt* bored into Kennedy Channel, which in places was only eleven miles wide and filled with heavy ice floating southward from the Arctic Ocean to Baffin Bay. The goal on this dangerous passage was Cape Sheridan where winter quarters would be established.

As soon as the *Roosevelt* entered the Arctic Circle, an imaginary circle about fifteen hundred miles from the North Pole, the crew was on a twenty-four-hour alert. The waters were filled with towering icebergs, and floating cakes of ice twenty feet thick and larger than a football field.

Constantly menaced by these death-dealing blocks of ice, the whaleboats on the *Roosevelt* were filled with emergency supplies and slung from their davits. Should the ship be crushed by ice and sunk, the whaleboats could be lowered in moments and the North Pole party and the crew could reach temporary safety. Any such emergency move would, of course, mean the end of the expedition.

On the fifth day, plowing northward through treacherous Kennedy Channel, two huge ice floes loomed dead ahead. The anxious crew saw them swing together like huge gates closing the channel against the oncoming *Roosevelt*.

Commander Peary leaped to the speaking tube connecting the bridge to the engine room.

"Chief," he shouted, "you've got to keep her moving."

"Aye, aye, sir," came the reply.

The *Roosevelt* shook and trembled like a living

thing as Chief Engineer Wardwell poured on the coal.

The ship drove forward. The ice floes drew closer and closer together. Now, only a thin thread of water remained of Kennedy Channel.

"You've got to jump her," Peary called to Wardwell. "Full speed ahead."

The *Roosevelt* hit the closing icy gate. Her bow rose like a submarine breaking water. It crashed down on the heavy ice, shattering it and widening the narrowed channel.

"More speed! More power!" Commander Peary shouted.

The ship groaned and strained. It was wedged in between the heavy ice floes. Engine failure, any failure meant the end. Open water was a quarter of a mile ahead. The water leading to it was no wider than a ditch. The ice floes, weighing thousands of tons more than the *Roosevelt,* continued their destructive pressure. At any second it seemed the ship would be forced out of the water and onto the surrounding ice, popped out like a piece of toast in a pop-up toaster.

"Man the lifeboats!"

The *Roosevelt* inched forward, shoving back the enemy ice.

A desperate thought pounded through Commander Peary's head. Was this the end? Would the increasing pressure of the ice from both sides knife through the ship, join at the ship's vitals, and hold her there suspended?

If this happened, Commander Peary knew, the *Roosevelt* would be lost. The ship would be held tightly in the ice. Its hull would fill with icy water. Days later, weeks later, even months later, when the ice floes separated, the *Roosevelt* would plunge to the bottom of the sea. The party would be saved, but all supplies would be lost and the expedition over.

But the sturdy *Roosevelt* rose to the occasion. She bucked and reared and drove against the closing ice. It took three hours to force the quarter mile of ever-narrowing ice until finally, with a gallant lcap, the ship broke out into open water.

Commander Peary turned and looked back. His eyes were met by a solid mass of ice—a solid mass which minutes before had been a narrow passage. Kennedy Channel was closed.

The *Roosevelt*, in open water at last, leaped forward like a frolicking puppy released from its leash. Robeson Channel lay ahead and beyond it, the Arctic Ocean.

Relief swept over the good ship *Roosevelt* like a hot shower.

Fears and worries were washed away. The stout ship bounced through the channel, banging away at smaller ice floes that cracked against her sides and smashed one lifeboat. A corner of a big berg cracked against the forward deck house, ripping part of it from the decking. But the commander and his crew were so happy at winning out over Kennedy Channel, these accidents seemed like nothing at all.

Rounding Cape Rawson, Cape Sheridan, where the party would set up winter quarters, came into view.

"My heart was light," Commander Peary wrote. "There are some feelings which a man cannot put into words. Such were mine as the mooring lines went out onto the ice foot at Cape Sheridan.

"Lying there, with the northern bounds of all known lands lying far to the south, we were in a position properly to attack the second part of our problem, the projection of a sledge party from the ship to the Pole itself."

It was now September 5, 1908. The long winter, the long night lasting over four months, was setting in. Not until the spring of 1909 could Commander Peary set out on his final dash for the Pole.

The winter was a busy one. Hunting parties went out daily for walrus and musk oxen to keep the party and the dogs supplied with meat. As the winter dragged toward its end, sledge parties hauled supplies over ninety miles of rugged ice to Cape Columbia. It was from this point that Commander Peary would make his strike due north over the ice to the Pole.

March 1, 1909, finally came—the day Commander Peary would leave camp for his "dash to the Pole."

Commander Peary arose early that morning. It was still quite dark, although the beginning light of the four-months-long day could already be seen. The arctic veteran ordered the trail-breaking parties to move out. He would bring up the rear to protect any member of his party who might run into serious trouble on the first of the daily "marches" toward the Pole.

He cast one last look at the camp. He turned his eyes northward. This was it. He had the dogs, the men, the experience, and the determination to win out. The end, as Commander Peary said, "lay with that Destiny which favors the man who follows his faith and his dream to the last breath."

Commander Peary divided his men into teams. One team would "march" for ten or twelve hours, or until exhaustion forced the team to halt. A second team would follow ten hours later, taking advantage of the path forged by the first team. On catching up, the second team would rest briefly, then march ahead, breaking the path for the first team. In this way, one team would be rested to pioneer a new trail while an exhausted team regained its strength.

Peary's party was composed of Matt Henson, Ootah, an Eskimo who had been with the commander on previous attempts on the Pole, and three Eskimo dog drivers. Peary would continue to march as the rear guard until the final dash. Then, as the other teams turned back, he would lead his party to the Pole.

The twenty-seventh march was the final one. It began on the thirty-sixth day after leaving Cape Columbia.

These "marches" were not easy sledding over smooth ice. They were tough battles every step of the way. The ice over the sea from Cape Columbia to the Pole resembles a field strewn with gigantic granite building blocks. Step by tortuous step, the dogs strained at the traces. Peary and the Eskimos heaved and shoved to get the sledges over the slippery, jagged, dangerous ice blocks. Some days, only a few miles were covered. On others, the commander would be cheered when he traveled as much as twenty-five miles.

On the fifth of April, Commander Peary took a latitude sight and knew he was only thirty-five miles from the Pole.

"I must make it by noon tomorrow," he told the others grimly.

He wanted to be at the Pole for a noon observation.

He ordered his men to rest. They would start the final dash at midnight. The men hastily constructed a snow igloo and turned in. Commander Peary strode back and forth in front of the igloo. His body ached in every bone. He was so tired he knew he must rest, and yet, when he finally lay down, sleep would not come. He was too near his goal, too near the victory that had escaped every man in history who had tried to grasp it.

By this time, the tall, broad-shouldered man looked more like a scarecrow. He had lost over thirty pounds. His clothes hung limply on him. His face was thin, his eyes deep-sunk in his face.

At midnight, he roused his companions. Although it was midnight, the sun was high overhead. This was the period of continuous daylight.

The final "dash" began. The party trudged steadily, wordlessly northward. A shrieking gale drove snow flurries and thin daggers of ice into their faces. On they went, step by step, stride by weary stride, nearer to the Pole.

Near the end of the first march of about ten miles, the party came upon a lead—open water —which was just beginning to spread.

"Hurry! Hurry!" shouted the commander.

Peary was first to leap on a cake of moving ice. He signaled his men. With a powerful shove, the commander leaped from the first cake of ice to another, shoving the first one backward so the other members of the team could scramble aboard it with the sledge and dogs. For one hundred yards, Peary and his men jumped from one cake of moving ice to another, trying desperately to reach the solid ice ahead.

The commander would leap on a piece of ice. He would test it to make sure the cake would not tilt under the weight of the dogs and sledge. Then he would leap back to the former cake where the dogs were and help the driver get dogs and the sledge to the tested ice cake ahead.

Finally, unbroken ice was reached. They had crossed the lead. Immediately, Commander Peary realized that instead of reaching the safety he felt sure was ahead, the party was in even more trouble. They had reached "young" ice, newly formed and so thin that it sagged beneath their weight. The commander was obliged to slide his feet, spreading them wide apart to distribute his own weight. He just made it to more solid ice. Other men in the party completed the dangerous crossing on all fours.

On April 6, 1909, at ten o'clock in the morning, Commander Peary ordered the party to halt.

Not a word was said as the commander took an observation. Breathless moments passed. Then, a slow smile spread across the explorer's cracked face.

"The Pole at last!" he said quietly. "The prize of three centuries. My dream and goal for twenty years. Mine at last!"

With these words, Commander Peary sank to the ice. In moments he was sound asleep.

The party remained at the Pole for thirty hours. Commander Peary, after planting the American flag on top of the world, started his homeward journey at four o'clock in the afternoon of April 7, 1909.

Robert E. Peary had done what no man had ever done before. The first man to reach the North Pole, he had conquered the blind, brute forces of nature where all others who had tried had failed.

Eleven Miles
to Life

The North Pole had been discovered. Commander Peary had reached it in April, 1909. Now explorers turned their eyes to the Antarctic. The South Pole, Latitude 90° South, became their new target.

Antarctica, at the bottom of the world, is completely different from the Arctic. The Arctic is a huge body of water and shifting ice packs, surrounded by land. The Antarctic is a huge area of ice-covered land, completely surrounded by water.

Temperatures at the South Pole are much lower than at the North. Readings of 80 degrees below zero have been taken in the summer months. In the winter the thermometer plunges below the minus 100-degree mark.

Antarctica is mountainous, rising ten thousand feet skyward. The blanket of ice which covers the area is 7,800 feet thick in certain places.

Danger comes not only from the ice, the snow, the blizzards, and the cold. It comes from the animals which roam the coasts of Antarctica. These are the killer whales which rove the seas in packs like wolves. In antarctic sailing directions, issued by the U.S. Navy, one sentence sums up the danger: "Killer whales will attack human beings at every opportunity."

The wolves of the sea even attack and kill the biggest of all animals—the blue whale. The blue whale at full growth weighs 150 tons!

Killer whales, about thirty feet long, swim deep. When they spot a shadow on the ice overhead, they rise swiftly, striking the ice with their backs, shattering it and spilling their dinner over the ice to be torn to shreds.

A photographer with the Scott Expedition spotted some killer whales along the shore in

McMurdo Sound. He ran to the edge of the ice
to take some pictures. He thought the whales had
vanished when:

I had got to within six feet of the edge
of the ice, about a yard thick, when, to
my consternation, it suddenly heaved
up under my feet and split into frag-
ments around me; whilst eight whales,
lined up side by side and almost touching each other, burst up from under the
ice and spouted.

The head of one was within two
yards of me. I saw its nostrils open, and
at such close quarters the release of its
pent-up breath was like a blast from an
air-compressor. I was enveloped in the
warm vapor of the nearest spout which
had a strong fishy smell. It was all I
could do to keep my feet as I leaped
from piece to piece of rocking ice with
the whales a few yards behind me, snort-

ing and blowing among ice blocks. I rec-
ollected distinctly thinking, if they did
get me, how very unpleasant the first
bite would feel, but that it would not
matter much about the second.

Two expeditions were being prepared and
equipped in 1910, in the months after the news
of Peary's success reached the world. One of
the expeditions headed by the Norwegian, Roald
Engelbregt Gravning Amundsen, had been
formed to go to the North Pole. When Amundsen heard that Peary had beaten him to it, he
quickly changed his plans. He would race the
Englishman, Robert Falcon Scott, to the South
Pole.

Amundsen's dash to the South Pole was comparatively easy. Scott's dash is one of the most
tragic tales ever told. It still lifts the hearts and
minds of men to hear of the pure heroism and
bravery of this gallant Englishman.

Interest in the South Pole hadn't appeared until the last five years of the nineteenth century. In 1895, the Sixth International Geographical Congress was held in London. At the end of its meetings, an announcement was made: "The exploration of the antarctic regions is the greatest piece of geographical exploration still to be undertaken." The Congress urged that nations and scientific societies promote expeditions to the Antarctic.

Several such expeditions were made around the turn of the century. None of them reached the South Pole. It began to appear that the South Pole might prove to be as difficult to reach as the North Pole had been.

Commander Peary did not agree, and he passed on his thinking to leaders of the two new expeditions getting under way. Peary pointed out that while the North Pole lies at the bottom of the sea two miles deep, the South Pole is on a plateau of land two miles high. This information he had gotten from previous expeditions that had tried to reach the South Pole. To reach the North Pole an expedition had to set out at the coldest time of the year, when the open water is covered by ice. On a march to the South Pole, the contrary is true. There is no open water. The ice is firm, resting on land, so a party can travel at the warmest time of the year.

Roald Amundsen studied Peary's statements carefully. He decided to move and move fast. He sailed from Norway to Greenland where he selected one hundred of the best dogs he could find. He then sailed south, setting up headquarters at the Bay of Whales across the Ross Sea from McMurdo Sound where Scott, heading the British expedition, had already established headquarters.

The race was on. The British had a head start. They left two weeks before the Norwegians set out for the South Pole.

Amundsen's party left the Bay of Whales, October 19, 1911. Five men made the dash in four sledges each drawn by thirteen dogs. They made excellent progress, covering ninety miles in the first four days.

The party traveled faster than any other polar expedition in history. By the end of one week, they had gone 340 miles and reached Latitude 85° 5′ South. They were nearing their goal.

Though Scott's party had left earlier they were traveling a longer route and their progress was much slower. At the expedition's sixty-seventh camp on January fifteenth, Scott wrote in the journal he kept:

> It is wonderful to think that two long marches would land us at the Pole. We left our depot today with nine days' provisions so that it ought to be a certain thing now, and the only appalling possibility would be the sight of the Norwegian flag forestalling ours. Only twenty-seven miles from the Pole.

Scott was worried. He felt sure that Amundsen's party was on its way, and the desire to beat the Norwegian was great.

Amundsen was making more rapid progress. He was carrying fewer supplies than Scott. The lighter load allowed the Norwegians to go at almost twice the speed of their British rivals. Amundsen could safely carry fewer supplies because of a polar technique he had adopted from another great Norwegian explorer, Fridtjof Nansen. The technique was to use the traveling dogs for food as the trip advanced. Each day as the party drew nearer and nearer to the Pole, a certain number of dogs would be killed and fed to the remaining dogs. No need, then, to carry extra food for the animals!

On the return trip, certain dogs could be slaughtered and used as food for the men. Again human food supplies could be cut down. Many polar explorers refused to adopt this plan. They became too fond of the dogs. But even though the plan might be revolting, it was effective.

As Amundsen himself put it, "What is death to one is food to another."

It was on January sixteenth, at camp sixty-eight, that Scott was forced to admit that he had lost. He wrote in his journal:

The worst has happened, or nearly the worst. We marched well in the morning and covered seven and one half miles. Noon sight showed us in Lat. 89° 42′ S., and we started off in high spirits in the afternoon, feeling that to-morrow would see us at our destination. About the second hour of the march, Bower's sharp eyes detected what he thought was a cairn. He was uneasy about it but argued that it must be a sastruga (a wavelike ridge of hard snow). Half an hour later he detected a black speck ahead. Soon we knew that this could not be a natural snow feature. We marched on, found that it was a black flag tied to a sledge bearer; nearby the remains of a camp, sledge tracks and ski tracks going and coming and the

clear trace of dogs' paws—many dogs.
This told us the whole story. The Norwegians have forestalled us and are first
at the Pole. It is a terrible disappointment, and I am very sorry for my loyal
companions. Many thoughts come and
much discussion have we had. Tomorrow we must march on to the Pole and
then hasten home with all the speed we
can compass. All the daydreams must
go; it will be a wearisome return.

Great God! This is an awful place
and terrible enough for us to have la-
boured to it without the reward of being
first.

Amundsen had won the race. He had reached
the South Pole on December 16, 1911, one full
month before the British, even though the Norwegians had started out two weeks after Scott.

As Scott had said, the dreams were gone. The
return was more than "wearisome." The story

of that return trip is one of the most heartbreaking ever told. Scott carefully recorded each horrible detail in his journal. The tragic words were printed after his death.

Even though the British explorer knew he was beaten, he and his party forged ahead and reached the Pole on January 19, 1912. They carried the Union Jack, England's flag, to a point three quarters of a mile north of the spot where the flag of Norway waved in the cold wind. "We have turned our back now on the goal of our ambition," Scott wrote, "and must face 800 miles of solid dragging—and good-bye to most of the daydreams!"

At first the party made fine progress. "It is warmer and pleasanter marching . . . I'm afraid the return journey is going to be dreadfully tiring and monotonous."

The weather worsened. Blizzards raged through the Antarctic. Temperatures dropped to 80 degrees below zero. Hands, feet, and faces became frozen. Food supplies grew shorter.

Two months of the brutal return trip had passed. They were nearing their haven, called One-Ton Depot. It was only fifteen miles away. If they could make it, then all would be safe. Only fifteen miles it was, but fifteen of the longest miles anyone ever tried to travel.

The most severe blizzard of them all struck the party. They were down to half a can of fuel. For four days they were unable to move. One member, Lawrence Oates, said he could not go on.

He proposed we should leave him in his sleeping bag. That we could not do, and we induced him to continue on the afternoon march. In spite of its awful nature for him, he struggled on and we made a few miles. At night he was worse and we knew the end had come.

An entry on March fourteenth told of this end:

Should this be found I want these facts recorded. Oates' last thoughts were of his mother, but immediately before he took pride in thinking that his regiment would be pleased with the bold way he met his death. We can testify to his bravery. He bore intense suffering for weeks without complaint. This was the end. He slept through the night before last hoping not to wake; but he woke in the morning—yesterday. It was blowing a blizzard. He said 'I am just going outside and may be some time.' He went out into the blizzard and we have not seen him since. We knew that poor Oates was walking to his death, but though we tried to dissuade him, we knew it was the act of a brave man and an English gentleman. We all hope to meet the end with a similar spirit, and assuredly the end is not far.

They were in a tent, only eleven miles from One-Ton Depot—only eleven miles from life! Scott was the last to die.

The following entries in his journal tell of that tragic end:

Thursday, March 22—Blizzard bad as ever—Wilson and Bowers unable to start—tomorrow last chance—no fuel and only one or two food left—must be near the end. Have decided it shall be natural—we shall march for the depot with or without our effects and die in our tracks.

March 29—Since the 21st we have had a continuous gale from W.S.W. and S.W. We have fuel to make two cups of tea apiece and bare food for two days on the 20th. Every day we have been ready to start for our depot 11 miles away, but outside the door of the tent it remains a scene of whirling drift. I do not think we can hope for any better things now. We shall stick it out to the end, but we are getting weaker, of course, and the end cannot be far.

It seems a pity, but I do not think I can write more. . . .

For God's sake look after our people.

R. Scott

The bodies of Scott and his companions were found in sleeping positions eight months later. Along with Scott's journal were found letters he had written to the relatives of his companions, expressing his great sympathy for them in the loss of their loved ones.

To the playwright Sir James M. Barrie, who was godfather to Scott's only son, he wrote:

> My Dear Barrie,
>
> We are pegging out in a very comfortless spot. Hoping this letter may be found and sent to you, I write a word of farewell. . . . More practically, I want you to help my widow and my boy— your godson. We are showing that Englishmen can still die with a bold spirit, fighting it out to the end. . . . Give the boy a chance in life if the State won't do it. He ought to have good stuff in him. Good-bye, my dear friend.
>
> Yours ever,
>
> R. Scott

Although Amundsen won the race, and Amundsen and Peary are considered among the greatest of polar explorers, the world regards Scott's last expedition as the noblest of them all.

From North Pole
to South

"Well done, young man. And where to now?"

The grizzled polar veteran, Roald Amundsen, clapped a hand on the shoulder of the younger explorer as he asked his question.

"The South Pole," Commander Richard Evelyn Byrd replied, half laughingly, half seriously.

It was the tenth of May, 1926, a memorable date in polar history. Commander Byrd had just completed man's first flight to the North Pole and back. On landing at Spitzbergen in the Norwegian islands of Svalbard, Byrd had been greeted by Amundsen whose arctic and antarctic expeditions had thrilled the world for thirty years. The torch of polar leadership was handed on at this meeting. Commander Byrd's exploits in Antarctica were to dominate polar exploration for the next thirty years, capturing wide public interest and adding to the world's knowledge of the vast icy regions.

Byrd's quick reply to Amundsen, made at the top of the world, was the commander's first public announcement of having set his sights on exploring the bottom of the world. He had been considering an antarctic expedition for several years, but not until his successful flight over the North Pole had tested and proven the airplane as a means of transportation in polar regions did he feel he could seriously start planning such a trip.

Amundsen took Byrd's reply in all seriousness and immediately agreed with him that the airplane was the new vehicle for polar exploration.

"The older order is changing," Amundsen said. "The airplane is the machine that can beat the Antarctic."

The two men, the young explorer and the veteran, discussed Byrd's proposed adventure far into the night. In his high enthusiasm, Amundsen offered the use of his own tested polar equipment. He gave Byrd the names of several fellow Norwegians who he felt would serve Byrd capably. He also named a ship, the *Samson,* as "the best bargain for that kind of a job you can find anywhere." Amundsen had used the stout barkentine *Samson* on polar explorations.

On an August afternoon in 1928, just two summers after Byrd's successful flight to the North Pole and his long conversation with Amundsen, the *Samson,* renamed the *City of New York,* slipped her moorings in New York harbor and Byrd's first antarctic expedition was on its way to the South Pole. The departure of the *City of New York* was cheered as the old windjammer was towed out of New York's harbor. Interest in Byrd's first expedition to the South Pole was as high as it had been for Peary's North Pole trip twenty years before.

Sixteen years had passed since anyone had

attempted to reach the South Pole. Amundsen, who led the first expedition to reach the South Pole, had made it in December, 1912. The British explorer, Robert Scott, had reached the Pole a month after Amundsen. Since that time, a world war had raged through Europe. Men had more immediate things to do than explore the far-off regions of the earth.

Byrd's South Pole expedition had been carefully planned with definite goals in mind. It was not to be just a dash to the Pole or a quick flight over it. The expedition would spend one year in Antarctica. Scientific studies would be made, including extensive weather observations and the charting of unknown lands.

The *City of New York,* purchased by Byrd at Amundsen's suggestion, was an old ship and a slow one. It would take her three months to make the trip from New York to Dunedin, New Zealand, the port from which the expedition would leave for the continent of Antarctica. Commander Byrd went on ahead by faster ship to make last minute arrangements and be ready to head for the Pole as soon as the *City of New York* arrived.

The old sailing vessel was a weird-looking ship as she wallowed in the waters of the port of Dunedin, heading out to sea from New Zealand eastward to the Ross Sea. New Zealanders shook their heads and didn't give the heavily loaded *City of New York* a chance of making the 2,500-mile trip to Antarctica safely. Her decks were piled high with airplanes, drums of gasoline, pre-fabricated houses, and crates of supplies. On top of all this, eighty-five sledge dogs barked and howled constantly.

Commander Byrd's destination was the Bay of Whales in the Ross Sea. The *City of New York* left Dunedin the second day of December, spent Christmas at sea and arrived in the Bay of Whales in early January. Near disaster greeted Byrd and the youngest member of his party before the staggering job of unloading the ship began. Byrd and Paul Siple, the nineteen-year-old Eagle Boy Scout chosen to go with the expedition, were in a small boat, moving through drifting ice cakes, looking for a place for the *City of New York* to heave to for unloading. Killer whales suddenly appeared, slicing through the floating ice, plowing up high wakes as they sped toward the small boat. If one of those killers struck the boat, it would heave it into the air as if it were a box of matches. The boat would crash and splinter on the jagged ice floes, and Byrd and Siple would be hurled into the icy waters. With the lead whale within just a few feet of the boat, Byrd and Siple leaped to a slab of ice jutting out from the shore into the Bay of Whales. Byrd whipped out his revolver and leveled it at the leader of the herd, but in that last moment the whales swerved away and headed out for deeper water.

"That was a close one, sir," Siple said to Commander Byrd.

"It surely was, Paul," Commander Byrd replied. He looked down at the revolver in his hand and smiled. "Don't know what good a shot from this thing would have done. A bullet would have been no more than a gnat bite to one of those whales."

Open water was found near the spot where the killer whales had attacked, and the *City of New York* was slowly edged shoreward through the ice. To anchor her securely, large iron hooks were planted in holes dug out of the ice that extended out from the shore and surrounded the ship. The landing had been made near the base set up years before by Roald Amundsen. As the *City of New York* was being unloaded, Byrd hunted for the remains of Amundsen's camp. But sixteen years of gales and snow and shifting ice had wiped away all traces of it. Byrd worked his way farther inland, and eight miles from the coast he found what he considered to be an ideal location for a permanent campsite.

Little America was born. That is the name Byrd gave to his Antarctic base. Buildings went up in a hurry and Little America soon looked like a miniature city. There were three main buildings: the administration building, the mess hall, and the Norwegian house (seven Norsemen, each suggested by Amundsen, were members of the expedition). There were dozens of smaller huts and three aircraft hangars.

Sledges pulled by dogs hauled 650 tons of supplies the eight miles from the Bay of Whales to Little America. The crates of supplies were stacked one atop the other in parallel walls. These were roofed over, providing weatherproof tunnels to connect the three main buildings.

Three weeks after landing at the Bay of Whales in January, 1929, the expedition began its work. The airplanes were warmed up and tested, and trial flights began. The long winter night was coming on; from April twenty-second to August twenty-second there would be no sunlight. Before the long night fell, the geologist, Lawrence Gould, wanted to get samples of rocks in the Rockefeller Mountains, a range discovered and named by Byrd on one of his first inland flights after establishing Little America.

Gould took off. The mission seemed to be

progressing smoothly because he radioed full reports daily. Then, without warning, transmission ceased and a worried Byrd led an air search party to find the geologist. Spotting a pin dot of light or a smoke signal from the air required constant, straining attention, but Byrd at last found these signs marking Gould's temporary campsite. As the plane swooped in, the rescuers could see Gould's Fokker plane upturned and wrecked a mile away.

"What happened?" Byrd asked when they had landed. The story the party told underlined the perpetual danger of the Antarctic.

"High winds came up," radio operator Harold June reported. "We lashed the plane down to moorings we had frozen into the ice. When the winds grew wilder, I climbed into the plane to make my daily radio report. When I looked at the speed indicator on the instrument panel it registered eighty-eight miles per hour even though the plane was tied down to the ice and not going anywhere. The plane kept rising and falling.

Larry came out to the plane, and when I looked out of the window I saw him hanging on to a rope attached to one of the wing tips. The wind was so strong it stretched his whole body straight out like a flag."

Sensing that the worst was yet to come, June and Gould had rushed back to the tent and dug themselves in just in time. The wind rose to a speed of 150 miles per hour. The plane broke its mooring lines. With its propeller whirling as if the engine were going, the pilotless plane took off, flew backward and crashed a mile away.

In carefully planned and skillfully executed ferry flights, necessary because Byrd's rescue plane could not carry all of them at once, Gould's party was taken back to Little America.

The long, long night set in. Even though there were comforts and amusements—books to read, games to play, plenty of food, clothing and warmth inside the main building—it was a trying time. As the weeks dragged on, the nerves of the forty-two men in the expedition began to fray.

Although all the men in the expedition were intelligent and dedicated to their task, the bleak monotony began to wear away their patience and twist their thinking. For example, one member refused to eat at the same table with another because his companion's chewing habits were annoying. More serious personal complications arose. Commander Byrd had to walk in the snow and bitter cold quietly reasoning with another man who thought he wanted to murder his closest friend. The man's ideas were hallucinations, of course, and Byrd finally talked him out of his weird desire.

When, at long last, the winter came to an end, Little America hummed with activity. The Ford Trimotor airplane was readied for Byrd's attempt to fly to the South Pole. Food, fuel, and other supplies were dropped on a food-laying flight to the foot of the Queen Maud Mountains. This precautionary measure was taken in the event the trimotor was forced down on either leg of its trip to the Pole. Life-sustaining supplies were stretched out over the icy miles between the camp at Little America and the South Pole.

On November 25, 1929, the heavily loaded trimotor took off with the veteran pilot Bernt Balchen at the controls. Byrd was the navigator; June, the radio operator; and Ashley McKinley, the co-pilot and cameraman.

Byrd was aiming for a pass between rugged mountain peaks called Liv Glacier. At the outset, the flight went smoothly, but as the plane darted into this giant chasm, the air roughened. The plane was tossed up and down and buffeted from side to side. Only Balchen's great skill as a pilot prevented it from crashing against the side of an ice-covered mountain.

Nearing the Pole, a huge mountain blocked the airplane. The altimeters showed the plane to be at 9,600 feet; this was near the plane's ceiling with its heavy load. The narrowing chasm directly ahead eliminated the possibility of turning around; they had to continue onward. Everyone in the aircraft knew that at least five hundred more feet of altitude was needed or they could not clear the peak.

In Commander Byrd's words:

> Balchen began to yell and gesticulate. It was hard to catch the words in the roar of the engines echoing from the cliffs on either side. But the meaning was manifest. 'Overboard—overboard —two hundred pounds!'

Which would it be—gasoline or food?

> If gasoline, I thought, we might as well stop there and turn back. We could never get back to the base from the Pole. If food, the lives of all of us would be jeopardized in the event of a forced landing.

The plane sped on through the narrow chasm. The menacing peak rushed toward them.

Was it fair to McKinley, Balchen, and June? It really took only a moment to reach a decision. The Pole, after all, was our objective. I knew the character of the three men. They were not so lightly to be turned aside. McKinley, in fact, had already hauled one of the food bags to the trap door.

One bag of food was not enough.

"More! More!" Balchen shouted.

Another bag of food shot through the trap door. The plane lifted and skimmed over the peak with less than five hundred feet to spare.

They reached the Pole in the next half hour. An American flag was dropped, weighted with a stone from the grave of Floyd Bennett who had flown Byrd over the North Pole.

The trip back to the base was smooth. All told, nineteen hours had elapsed from take-off to touchdown.

News of Byrd's successful flight to the South

Pole was radioed to New York and flashed throughout the world. The North Pole and the South Pole had been conquered by air, and by the same man. On the expedition's return to New York, Byrd and his party were given a hero's welcome with a ticker tape parade up Broadway from the Battery. The Congress of the United States expressed the nation's gratitude for Byrd's achievements by making him a rear admiral.

Two years later, in the fall of 1933, Admiral Byrd was on his way to the South Pole once again. On this trip, Byrd spent six months alone in a hut just short of the South Pole. He had planned to "winter over" as near the South Pole as possible. He had two reasons for this. One, he wanted to study the weather near the South Pole during the six-months period of continuous darkness. He also wanted to test how man would be affected by spending six months in complete isolation in the most desolate part of the world.

For the first months, Byrd kept radio communication with the base at Little America, sending back meteorological reports daily. Temperatures outside his small hut dropped to 100 degrees below zero. It was a lonely six months for the explorer, with the threat of death always present.

Toward the end of the second month, Byrd was overcome by carbon monoxide gas as he was repairing the gasoline generator which powered his radio transmitter. He never fully recovered from this experience during the rest of his long and lonely vigil. From time to time there were periods when he was unable to keep any food in his stomach. On several occasions, fumes from his small kerosene heater overcame him. Finally, he became so weak that he was no longer able to crank the hand generator to power transmission back to Little America. The gasoline generator had failed.

Back at the base, alarm grew at the cessation of transmission from Admiral Byrd. As the days became weeks, with the weather still so bad that it was impossible to launch an airplane to go to Byrd's rescue, a snowmobile was equipped and a search party set out overland to rescue the expedition leader.

Admiral Byrd felt a searching party must be on its way to his rescue so he conserved his remaining strength for the one task which would save his life. Each day he staggered out of his hut, attached a flare to a kite, lighted it, and sent the kite into the sky as a beacon to guide the rescuers to his hut.

After many days, Byrd finally spotted the snowmobile in the distance, but to his despair, it appeared to be veering away from the path leading to the hut. Snow flurries cut off vision between him and his rescuers, and he feared that, having come this close, they were not going to find him.

With his last flare, Byrd sent his kite skyward. The flare was spotted and the rescue party came rushing up to Byrd's hut.

The rescuers were shocked by Byrd's appearance. He was hollow-cheeked, and so thin the wind staggered his body, but there was triumph in his voice as he told the rescue party, "The meteorological records are complete."

The rescuers stayed with Byrd in a hastily built camp by the hut for two months, until their leader had recovered sufficient strength to make the return trip to the base. When weather conditions permitted, an airplane flew out to take Byrd back to Little America.

In 1957, Admiral Byrd was named by President Eisenhower as Officer in Charge of the United States Antarctic Program for the International Geophysical Year. Unable because of his health to head the United States' expedition to the South Pole in person, Byrd named as his deputy a man who had gone with him on his first expedition to the South Pole, almost thirty years before. The man had been only a boy then, Eagle Scout Paul Siple, the lad who had been with Byrd when the admiral's polar career had almost ended with an attack of killer whales in the Bay of Whales.

The Voyage
of the *Italia*

"The *Italia* is now officially missing. Nobile and seventeen men aboard. The Italian Government formally requests Norway to aid in the search."

This telegram was handed a grizzled veteran of arctic and antarctic exploration.

"Sir, our ministry asks if you would undertake to head up the search."

Many thoughts raced through the veteran's mind before he replied. The situation was extremely ironic. He was being asked to search for and save the life of a man who had heaped abuse on him; a man who had ridiculed the polar explorer's abilities.

Roald Amundsen, the great Norwegian polar

explorer, discoverer of the South Pole, one of two men who had reached both Poles, looked up at the messenger. A slight smile flashed across his leathery face.

"I can be ready at once," he replied in a soft voice.

Two years before, Amundsen had flown over the North Pole in the dirigible *Norge*, commanded by the Italian General Humberto Nobile. The flight was hailed around the world, with most of the praise directed at the great explorer Amundsen. Nobile was furious. He fired his first blast:

"The real credit for the success of the flight belongs to the man who piloted the airship so skillfully." He was referring to himself. "Not to the man who sat idly in the gondola, looking out the window."

Amundsen did not reply to this charge at once. Nobile kept up his biting remarks. Amundsen was forced to reply.

"On three occasions," he announced, "Nobile

nearly wrecked the *Norge* due to inexpert maneuvering. He made dangerous errors in navigation. He knows nothing of polar conditions. He is a braggart."

Nobile continued his insults. Amundsen refused further reply.

World opinion was with Amundsen, and this infuriated Nobile even more. He would show the world. He would show up Amundsen. He would go to the Pole again. This time the ship, instead of being called the *Norge,* or Norway, would be called the *Italia* for Italy, and it would be manned by an Italian crew.

This second voyage, of no real scientific value, set into action a chain of events which brought about feuding among four nations. Heroic men of France, Norway, and Sweden lost their lives in the search for Nobile. Only seven of the eighteen who ventured forth on the *Italia* came back alive.

The voyage, the search, and the bitter disputes following shocked the world.

The impetuous, headstrong Nobile did show

a little caution. He decided to add the Swedish scientist and explorer Finn Malmgren to his expedition. He also asked advice from the dean of all polar explorers, Amundsen's fellow countryman, Fridtjof Nansen. Nansen, still strong at eighty-seven, gave the advice gladly.

"Take dogs. Very valuable. Even in the cooking pot."

Nansen had developed the technique of using dogs not only to pull the sledges, but for food if supplies ran out.

Nobile did not take his advice. He felt, and rightly so, that the dogs would take up too much room in the *Italia's* small gondolas.

The start of the disastrous trip took place April 14, 1928. The *Italia* slipped her mooring in Milan and headed north. She flew to Spitsbergen in short hops, arriving the first week in May.

Once at this northern island, Nobile's impatience seemed to slacken. The period of heavy fog was drawing near. He made two trial flights. Time was growing short, but still he delayed the departure. He even suggested postponing the flight until the fall.

"Out of the question," the Swedish scientist Malmgren replied. "I've got to be back in Sweden by the first of August."

Nobile knew he had to have Malmgren along. He was the only man with any polar experience. If trouble came, if the *Italia* were forced down, Malmgren's experience might lead them to safety.

"We take off tomorrow, May twenty-third," Nobile commanded.

The three motors of the *Italia* were warmed up early in the morning.

"Cast off!" came the command. The *Italia* rose slowly in the dawn. It was four thirty in the morning. The nose of the airship was pointed toward the North Pole, a thousand miles away.

The cold green waters of the Arctic Ocean passed swiftly below. The waters became flaked with blocks of ice. The airship droned on. Solid ice appeared below. They were approaching the ice pack which covers the top of the earth.

The navigator estimated the distance remaining to the Pole.

"Sixty miles, sir," he reported to Nobile.

Excitement was growing. Nobile's face wore an expression of triumph.

"Heavy clouds ahead," came another report.

Nobile scanned the skies with his binoculars. Would it be wise to chance the expedition's safety by running into that thick curtain of black clouds?

"What's our position now?" he asked.

"A few minutes north of latitude eighty-nine."

Nobile decided to risk it. The *Italia* plunged into the menacing bank of clouds. It was as dark as night.

At exactly midnight, the airship shot out of the clouds. The sun was shining brightly. The navigator shot the sun with his sextant.

"Latitude eighty-nine thirty," he chanted.

The *Italia* was speeding toward the Pole at forty miles an hour. In twenty minutes she would be over her goal.

"We're going to make it!" Nobile cried.

The airship's three motors throbbed.

"Latitude ninety degrees," the navigator called out calmly.

"We've made it! We've made it!" Nobile exulted.

The airship's motors were cut. The *Italia* drifted to a stop and hovered directly over the North Pole.

Nobile's dream had come true. He had shown the world and had demonstrated that he did not need Amundsen. His elation knew no limits.

The *Italia* began circling the Pole. Nobile wanted to descend and land; that would really be outdoing Amundsen. But the maneuver would have been a very dangerous one, and he was persuaded not to attempt it.

Once more the *Italia's* motors were cut. The ship hovered four hundred feet over the Pole. Nobile had a crewman bring him an oaken cross given him at an audience with Pope Pius XI just before he left on his expedition.

The cross and the Italian flag were dropped

from a gondola window. The cross plunged straight downward, landing upright in a snow bank. The flag fluttered, the banner streaming upward from the flagpole. It struck pole down, wavered, then fell over on its side.

Messages cracked through the night—messages of triumph to the Pope, to King Victor Emmanuel, and to *Il Duce,* Benito Mussolini.

The *Italia's* motors were started up again and the airship pointed toward Spitsbergen. It was then that the jubilation of the great moment began to fade.

Almost immediately the craft was engulfed in heavy mist and dense fog. A strong wind blew up out of the west, driving the *Italia* off her course. In spite of the thrust of the ship's three motors, she was whipped and spun about in the swirling winds and inky blackness.

The *Italia* had made the trip to the Pole in twenty-two hours. Now, on her return, twenty-four hours had already passed. Using the directional wireless on the *Italia* to his supply ship,

Citta di Milano, in Spitsbergen, Nobile had a line on his position, but did not know exactly *where* along that line he was! The ship was lost.

The *Italia's* wireless operator, Giuseppe Biagi, worked his instrument frantically, pouring urgent demands into the ears of the wireless operators aboard the *Citta di Milano.*

"Our position? Where are we? Where are we?" Biagi tapped out this signal again and again. "Position? Where . . ."

A shout cut short Biagi's wireless transmission. Near panic swept through the ship.

"The elevators are jammed!" The cry was terrifying to all aboard because the elevators controlled the dirigible's rise and descent.

The *Italia* plunged down through the thick mists toward the jagged ice below. She dropped to three hundred feet. Spikes of ice rising thirty feet could be clearly seen. The dirigible would be cut to pieces if she hit. But at 150 feet, the sickening plunge was slowed. At one hundred feet above ground, the descent halted. Miraculously, the ship was caught in a strong updraft of wind and began to rise. Mechanics worked feverishly to repair the elevators, but an hour later, the *Italia* was in trouble again. She started sinking downward, tail first, with increasing speed.

Sixty feet . . . forty . . . thirty . . . ! Down she plunged! Everyone aboard prayed that death would come quickly.

With a thunderous burst, the *Italia* struck the jagged ice.

Nobile was thrown clear of the ship. He lay on the ice, his right leg and right arm broken, and awaited the end that seemed inevitable. After a while, when consciousness persisted, he groaned and raised himself slightly. He could not believe his eyes. The *Italia* was in the air! Her tail was down and ropes and cables streamed from her bottom, but she was airborne and drifting away to the east.

Nobile groaned and his moan of pain was answered by others. When he looked about him, he saw that eight of his companions had survived the crash with him. Two were already on their feet staring at the departing *Italia*. The body of the only man killed in the crash lay fifty feet away from the others.

The crash survivors watched until the *Italia* drifted out of sight—forever. The men on the ground knew what had happened. When the airship hit the ice, the impact had sheared off the main gondola containing Nobile and the others. With this lightening of the craft's load she rose again, taking eight men in the other gondola with her.

Nine men had survived the crash. Their joy at being alive faded with the disappearing airship. How would they get back to civilization? Spitzbergen was a month's trek away. What would they use for shelter? How could they communicate with the world they had left behind? These were the troubled questions the surviviors asked themselves as they watched the *Italia* fade out of sight in the whirling mists.

Nobile closed his eyes. He was ready to die. His

thoughts went back to the advice given him by Nansen, the advice he had ignored. There were no dogs along. Others in the group moved about, searching the wreckage strewn over the ice. They found a tent, clothing, and signal rockets.

A shout of joy came from the wireless operator Biagi.

"I've found it!" He had found the portable wireless set—their only link to civilization— undamaged.

The red emergency tent was hurriedly erected and the wireless antenna rigged to its top. Biagi banged out Nobile's appeal for aid, stating their estimated position. All huddled around Biagi, waiting for the reply that was soon to come:

"*Italia*. Courage. Coming your assistance."

The men cheered, hugged one another, and danced on the snow-covered ice. They were saved. That was what they thought at first. But this same message was repeated again and again. Biagi was puzzled. So were Nobile and the others.

"They're not receiving us, General," Biagi said.

"They keep sending the same message. They haven't said a thing about receiving my message. They haven't asked any questions about survivors or our condition."

Biagi sent his message again.

The same reply came back:

"*Italia*. Courage. Coming your assistance."

Biagi changed his message.

"S.O.S. *Italia,* near Foyn Island. Our position is ..."

Every hour, as agreed with the *Citta di Milano* before departure, Biagi sent out his plea: "S.O.S. *Italia*. We are on drift ice. Position constantly changing. We need food, batteries. ..." Switching to his receiving channel, Biagi and the others were shocked when they heard a radio news broadcast: "Continued silence convinces us that the *Italia* is lost. Can there be any survivors?"

Neither Biagi nor any of the others could understand why their signal was not being heard, but they knew they were not getting through because the *Citta di Milano* kept sending out the same message. The *Milano's* repetitious call had been sent out with the forlorn hope that the Nobile party might hear the message and know that all efforts were being made to locate the men.

Days passed with no indication that the messages Biagi continued sending out were heard. A three-man party—Finn Malmgren, the Swedish scientist, and two Italian naval officers, Adalperto Mariano and Filippo Zappi—started out on foot to reach the shore and help. They did not know it then, but their expedition would create still another fantastic episode in the shocking log of the *Italia's* voyage.

The batteries of the portable wireless were weakening, but Biagi continued to tap out his message. On the sixth of June, almost two weeks after the crash, Biagi was taking down a news report from a short-wave station in São Paulo, thousands of miles south in warm and sunny Brazil. Excitement began to show on Biagi's face.

"We've been heard!" he shouted. He continued scribbling, tore the message off his pad, and

handed it to Nobile. The news was that a short-
wave amateur in Russia had received Biagi's
message and transmitted it to the Italian ambas-
sador in Moscow.

Hopes rose again.

It was two days later that the *Citta di Milano*
acknowledged receiving Biagi's message. The
Nobile survivors felt certain they were saved now.
Rescue operations would begin at last.

As soon as the Italian government had officially announced that Nobile and his party were
missing, rumors as to the *Italia's* whereabouts
flashed around the world. An American news-
paper falsely reported the *Italia* landing in
Alaska. Seal hunters reported seeing distress signals on Amsterdam Island, just north of Spitsbergen. A ship sped to the scene and found the
island deserted.

From Altoona, Pennsylvania, a short-wave
amateur reported receiving a message: "S.O.S. No
shelter except that offered by wreck of airship.

Position: Latitude 84° 15′ 06″ North; Longitude 15° 02′ East." The report appeared to be a hoax. The *Italia's* last message when she was desperately calling for her position showed her to be in the vicinity of 80° North. She couldn't possibly have drifted as far north as Latitude 84,° but there was no way of checking.

While the nine survivors sat on the ice sending an unheard signal, rumors, false messages, and weird reports continued. They were widely printed and eagerly consumed by an excited, curious public. World attention was divided between Spitsbergen and Tromsö on the north coast of Norway where Amundsen had gone after signifying his willingness to hunt for Nobile. Amundsen would launch his rescue attempt from Tromsö, a harbor on the Arctic Ocean about a thousand miles from Spitsbergen. During the period when wild rumors about the *Italia* were flying about, Amundsen was trying desperatcly to sccure suitable transportation for use in his search. He cabled his American friend and fellow explorer, Lincoln

Ellsworth, for help. Ellsworth had flown Amundsen on arctic flights before. But there was no reply, because Ellsworth was off on an exploration.

While waiting for Ellsworth's reply, the news was flashed to Tromsö that definite communications with Nobile had been established. Even with true reports winging in from Nobile, confusion and suspicion still clouded the picture. The Italian government, for no understandable reason, concealed part of the truth. It first announced that all members of the expedition were safe. This announcement was followed by one stating that the *Italia* had disappeared with half its crew aboard.

Wireless operators knew that Nobile and his group were on drift ice because the position from which their messages were coming was changing daily. How could they be rescued? They had no sledges, no dogs, no skis.

Again Amundsen's advice was sought as he waited in Tromsö for Ellsworth's reply.

"The survivors are in danger," he told newsmen. "The polar drift is carrying them farther and farther away. We need the big hydroplane I've asked Ellsworth for. The icebreaker may be too late. Remember, they have no food supplies."

The icebreaker Amundsen referred to was the Russian vessel *Krassin,* the most powerful icebreaker in Europe. The *Krassin* had sailed from Tromsö a few days before to search the area where reports from Nobile were coming. Little attention was paid to the *Krassin's* sailing as all eyes were focused on Amundsen. Within two weeks, though, the *Krassin* was to assume a role of major importance.

Suitable transportation was offered Amundsen from an unexpected source and he seized upon it happily. The French government had been experimenting with a long-distance hydroplane, the *Latham 47,* and offered it and its crew to Amundsen.

The *Latham* arrived in Tromsö on June sixteenth, by which date the *Italia* had been missing for twenty-four days. Amundsen boarded the plane immediately for an inspection tour, and the plane was loaded and prepared for a take-off for the following day, June twenty-seventh, at four o'clock.

Cheers rocked the skies over Tromsö harbor as Amundsen stepped into the *Latham* to take off on his search for the man who had scorned him. He was a national hero in Norway, a hero around the world.

At five o'clock the hydroplane flew over the Ekhingen Lighthouse where a geophysical institute station was maintained to send out weather reports to fishing vessels. Gilbert Brazy, the radio operator on the *Latham,* kept in constant contact with the lighthouse. At seven thirty the lighthouse radio operator cut off communication to send out his weather reports to the fishing fleet. Half an hour later he called the *Latham* again.

"Calling *Latham*. Calling *Latham*. Can you read me? Report your position."

He waited.

"Calling *Latham*," he repeated. "Answer, please. Answer."

There was no answer. There would be none.

Amundsen had given his life to rescue Nobile. Never again was Norway to see her heroic son.

The world was shocked when it learned of the disappearance of the famed explorer. The world was also angered. It resented Amundsen's giving up his life for a man who had said so many harsh things about him.

Many Norwegians refused to believe Amundsen was lost. Search and rescue parties were quickly formed. The waters around Spitsbergen were crisscrossed in the hope of finding the *Latham* downed but riding the cold seas.

News of Amundsen's disappearance reached the Russian icebreaker *Krassin* as she steamed steadily toward Spitsbergen. Professor Samoilovitch, in charge of the Russian rescue expedition, immediately shifted course to join in the search although he knew he could not devote too much time to this new disaster. His orders were to bring back Nobile; others would carry the main burden of the Amundsen search. As the ship nosed through the dark waters, heavy fog closed in. It became impossible to spot any object more than one hundred feet away from the *Krassin*. Her horn bellowed out a weird sound over the waters, punctuated by silence. If the *Latham* were anywhere nearby, the survivors would surely give an answering shout. None came, and after several hours the *Krassin* abandoned the search and re-set her course for Spitsbergen.

Just north of Spitsbergen, on the thirtieth of June, Professor Samoilovitch was astounded and shocked when his radio operator brought him a dispatch. *It was from General Nobile.* He requested permission to join the *Krassin* in its search for the remaining survivors of the *Italia.*

At first the professor thought the radiogram might be a hoax. Yet he knew it could not be. Apparently General Nobile, and only he, had been rescued. How could this have happened?

The whole world was asking the same question.

Disgrace was beginning to settle over the Nobile Expedition.

The rescue of Nobile, surrounded as it was with criticism of the general, also startled the world since it came from a completely unexpected source. A Swedish aviator and soldier of fortune, Einar-Paal Lundborg, came out of nowhere to fly to Nobile's aid. Lundborg, who loved the spotlight, decided that while the *Krassin* plodded slowly to the scene and the Italian supply ship remained at anchor, *he* would rescue Nobile.

In a light Fokker equipped with ski runners, he flew to Spitsbergen and took off from that base heading northeast toward the last reported position of the survivors. Lundborg located the red tent, landed on a rough strip prepared by the survivors, and took Nobile off the ice floe. On his return to pick up others, Lundborg crashed and became a prisoner on the same floe from which he had rescued Nobile.

The world pressed the question: How could the leader of an expedition permit his own rescue while his comrades were still in danger? The situation was compared to the abandoning of a sinking ship by its captain—leaving crew and passengers behind.

In defense of Nobile, it must be said that reports following his rescue were to the effect that he did not want to be the first man taken off. The stories were confusing and what really happened has never become clear.

One report was that Lundborg insisted Nobile come first because he was injured. But there were others injured. Another report had it that Lundborg insisted that he was under orders to take Nobile because the general would be of assistance in guiding the rescue of the others and in directing the search for Malmgren, Mariano, and Zappi, the three who had set out on foot. It was denied later that Lundborg had any orders, and some believed Lundborg wanted to rescue Nobile first only for the glory of bringing out the leader of the expedition.

Whatever the reasons, Nobile was to regret

for the rest of his life that he permitted himself to be the first man taken off. Ten days later, a week after he had radioed the *Krassin,* criticism of his action had become so widespread and so intense that Nobile was placed under arrest and made a prisoner in his own cabin.

Professor Samoilovitch had ignored Nobile's radiogram in any event. Precious time would have been lost in putting in to Spitsbergen to pick up Nobile. The *Krassin* was kept on her course toward the area where the remaining survivors were adrift on the ice floe. Samoilovitch dispatched the icebreaker's plane to expand the search. It was difficult to determine an exact position since the ice floe was drifting rapidly.

Aboard the *Krassin,* word from the Russian aviator Tchuknovski was anxiously awaited. Two hours passed. A message winged through the air to the aviator.

"We wait for you. Reply."

There was no answer.

Just as the *Krassin* was about to give up hope

for its aviator, a message came through.

"Group Malmgren. Charles."

At first this message was puzzling, but Professor Samoilovitch finally figured it out. It must mean that Tchuknovski had spotted the Swedish scientist Malmgren and the two Italian naval officers, Zappi and Mariano. They must be on Charles XII Island in the Arctic Ocean west of Spitsbergen.

What about Tchuknovski? Had he crashed? Two hours later came word that he had been forced down near Cape Wrede, but he and his companions were safe.

The *Krassin* sped toward Charles XII Island. As they neared it, a shout went up from the lookout in the crow's nest. He had spotted human figures staggering toward the shore, waving their arms.

Samoilovitch picked up his binoculars. He saw the figures. But only two. There were supposed to be three.

A small boat was launched. The two survivors

were picked up and brought aboard. One was Zappi, the other Mariano.

Samoilovitch questioned them. "And Malmgren? What happened to him?"

At first the Italians were evasive. Samoilovitch put pressure on them.

"He died. He was weak. He couldn't make it. He gave me his compass," Zappi said. "He asked us to dig him a grave so he could crawl into it to die."

Samoilovitch was suspicious. Zappi was wearing not only his own clothes but Malmgren's as well.

"Malmgren was alive when you left him?"

The Italians nodded their heads.

"He made us go."

Samoilovitch could get no more from the men.

Ugly guesses about what had actually happened spread fast when the world learned this shocking news. Malmgren was an experienced polar explorer. He was a strong man, a young man. Zappi and Mariano for years continued to tell the same story, and there was no one to prove they were lying, but the world had its doubts.

Samoilovitch put the *Krassin* on a course for the last reported position of the ice floe. A day later the remaining survivors and the aviator Lundborg were taken off.

There were still many questions asked, and few were answered. The *London Daily News* demanded an investigation:

> The somber North Pole drama the whole world has followed with such painful interest has certain elements of mystery. The best way to clear up the whole matter and restore the good name of the parties concerned would be to institute an impartial investigation as speedily as possible.

Protests and demands for an investigation came from Denmark and Sweden. In Germany, a cartoon was published showing Nobile, Zappi, and Mariano with teeth bared behind bars. The caption on the cartoon was one word: "Cannibals."

Italy refused to take any action. The Italian government would make its own investigation but would permit no outside observers.

Months passed. Nobile was dropped from the army, stripped of his title. Zappi and Mariano were heard of no more.

The sorry saga of the *Italia* was closed.

It had cost the lives of many men, including that of Roald Amundsen, one of the world's greatest explorers. It had been begun in bitterness, had been the cause of a most painful tragedy, and would remain shrouded in mystery forever.

Crash in the Antarctic

"Let's get out of here! And fast!"

The pilot put the plane in a long, sweeping left turn. The huge aircraft lost altitude. There was a sharp jolt. The plane had struck an ice hump. The pilot gunned the engines, trying for more altitude. Seconds passed. The plane struggled upward. Then it exploded. Bodies of men went hurtling through the air and plunged downward into the snow.

This tragic accident, the most serious of a number which were to beset Operation Highjump, brought about one of the most dramatic rescues in the history of polar exploration.

Operation Highjump began in 1946. It was

conceived by the United States Navy as an airborne expedition to the Antarctic. Extensive photo-maps were to be made. Men were to be trained under polar conditions. Snow and ice runways were to be constructed. Tests were to be run to see if the ice was thick enough to support a heavily loaded Globemaster, the largest of all cargo-transport planes.

The directive making Highjump operational ended with the words: ". . . with particular attention to later application of such techniques to operations in interior Greenland."

Thirteen ships and 4,000 men steamed south to put Highjump into operation. This was the largest polar expedition ever mounted.

One of these ships was the seaplane tender *Pine Island*. She lay in an open lagoon, surrounded by ice-filled waters, a thousand miles east of Little America. Two giant Martin Mariner seaplanes were lowered into the water. It was a tricky maneuver. The *Pine Island* heeled over from the weight of the plane as each of them was lowered over the side.

Martin Mariners, called PBM's by navy men, had proven themselves during the war in the South Pacific, searching for Japanese warships. Now they would be flying on a different search, seeking out new glaciers, islands, and mountains.

One of the Mariners, called *George One* for radio communication purposes, roared into the sky early in the morning of December thirtieth. Forty-five minutes later Radioman Wendell K. Hendersin sent out a message:

CEILING 500 TO 1000 FEET SKY COM-
PLETELY OVERCAST OBJECTS NOT VISI-
BLE TWO MILES SNOW OR SLEET WIND
SOUTH 11 TO 16 KNOTS.

That was the last communication received by the *Pine Island* from *George One*.

The weather closed in. A cloak of snow cut visibility to under three hundred feet. No plane could possibly take off to search for the missing *George One*.

Eleven days passed before the weather lifted sufficiently for a search to begin. A light plane rose from the water. Four hours later it messaged back:

MARINER GEORGE ONE BURNT WRECK-AGE AND ALIVE MEN AT 71.03 SOUTH 98.47 WEST.

Minutes later came a second radio message:

LOPEZ HENDERSIN WILLIAMS DEAD. SIX OTHERS ALIVE AND ON FEET. PLANE DIS-INTEGRATED AND BURNED.

Lieutenant J. L. Ball, pilot of the search plane, wrote a note telling the downed men about water to their north and asked them if they could travel on foot. If they could, they should form a circle; if not, a straight line. He swooped low and hurled the message out in a sardine can.

The search plane circled and came back over a ring of men who with "joined hands, danced and stood on their heads."

Lieutenant Ball returned to the *Pine Island* at full throttle.

When the *George One* struck the icecap, it was torn apart. Lieutenant William H. Kearns, the co-pilot, was flying the plane. He shot up through the cockpit windshield. He had failed to fasten his seat belt. The pilot, Lieutenant Ralph Paul "Frenchy" LeBlanc, was strapped in.

Kearns stumbled to his feet in a snowbank. He heard screams of pain coming from the shattered plane. The aircraft was on fire, and Frenchy LeBlanc was still strapped in. Kearns rushed back to the plane. Ignoring the scorching flames, he helped LeBlanc free himself and dragged him from the craft. Kearns did not realize that his right arm had been broken in the crash. Since he could not move it, he used his left arm in freeing his flying mate. Only when LeBlanc was safe did Kearns feel the throbbing pain extending from his fingertips to his shoulder.

When the plane exploded, the nose section had

flown off with Captain Henry H. Caldwell in it. Captain Caldwell was skipper of the *Pine Island* and had come along for the ride.

Part of the plane was intact—the fuselage, and the long tunnel leading from the cockpit to the tail. LeBlanc was carried into the tunnel and covered with parachutes.

There were six survivors of the crash— LeBlanc, Kearns, Caldwell, Radioman Third Class James Robbins, Aviation Machinist's Mate William Warr, and Owen McCarthy, Chief Photographer's Mate, lying unconscious in the snow.

Warr and Robbins were in good shape compared to the others. They searched for useful items which would soon become buried in the drifting snow. The medical supplies were nearly all gone, burned in the fire. They did find about two hundred pounds of pemmican and 350 cans of lifeboat rations.

Suddenly Warr and Robbins dropped in their tracks. They had ridden themselves to the limit, spurred on by the uncontrollable energy which came to them from the shock of the crash. They crawled into the tunnel, snuggled in between the others, and for a day and a half the six men lay in the tunnel in the stupor of exhaustion.

The bitter cold finally stirred them to action. They were all wearing electrically heated flying suits. With no current, these light suits gave them little protection from the cold.

It was New Year's Eve when Robbins and Warr came out of the shock and exhaustion which had hit the men. They found the plane's cockpit, now partly buried in the snow. They discovered some canned goods, including a can of apricots. They opened the can and each took out two halves of apricots.

"Happy New Year, Warr."

"Happy New Year, Robbins."

It was the first food the men had had since leaving the *Pine Island*.

The search for food became a game. All felt they would be rescued, but no one knew when a plane would come. They had to find food and ration it against a long wait in the cold and snow.

More food was found: butter, dill pickles, raw potatoes, canned peaches, a ham, bacon, and some fresh beefsteaks.

Even with what appeared to be plenty of food, the six survivors rationed themselves to two meals a day.

By the end of the first week, the men had regained sufficient strength to bury their three dead comrades. These were the first Americans to die on the continent of Antarctica. They were buried under the starboard wing of the plane and a flag placed at the head of their graves.

The long wait began. There was nothing to do. They did not know that open water was just ten miles away, but even if they had, their inflatable life rafts would have been of little use to them there. Where would they go in the choppy, ice-floe-strewn Bellingshausen Sea, far within the Antarctic Circle?

To break up the endless monotony of waiting, a game of checkers was devised. Malt discs were used for the black men and white candy squares for the red men.

The crew of the *Pine Island* worried and fumed as the weather prevented an early search. In the meantime the six survivors, experienced airmen, knew they could not expect a rescue until the skies had cleared.

It was a matter of desperate importance that they find some method of sending a signal to the *Pine Island* to give the tender their position. It was Robbins who made the lucky discovery, a "Gibson Girl," the name for an emergency, hand-cranked radio transmitter. They rigged and flew the kite designed to carry the antenna and began cranking away, tapping out their position. They had no way of knowing if they were being received.

Cranking the "Gibson Girl" was an exhausting operation. After an hour they stopped. They were too tired to pull down the kite. The wind snatched at it, broke it loose, and carried it away.

The next day they rigged a second antenna to

the highest part of the crashed plane and sent out their signal again.

Captain Caldwell began keeping a diary:

"The sky is down on us today," he wrote of the eighth day following the crash.

Ninth day: "There is no flying on such a day as this so we have very little to look forward to. Such days really drag on interminably."

Tenth day: "Half a slice of bread and peanut butter for breakfast."

Eleventh day: "Good day today. Visibility excellent, low broken clouds—much blue sky."

The spirits of the group rose with the lifting weather. They shot even higher when Lieutenant Ball's plane came into sight and the message in a sardine can came hurtling down. That was when they danced and stood on their heads.

The twelfth day passed with everyone keeping his eyes turned skyward. But no plane came into sight. They weren't worried, but they wondered why a plane had not returned to get them. Frenchy LeBlanc was dangerously ill. He had developed gangrene in both feet and had been delirious for days, calling out again and again for a doctor.

On the thirteenth day the second Martin Mariner came into sight.

"Everyone shouted," Kearns wrote later. "Bill Warr waved the brightest colored cloth he could find, an orange life-raft cover. Robbins fired the Very pistol. McCarthy set off the smoke grenades."

But the hopes of the party were plunged to

the depths. The plane flew right over them, continuing on a straight course with no wing-dipping acknowledgment that it had spotted them.

Two hours later they heard the drone of the Mariner's engines on its return flight. During the wait, they had made a pyre from parts of the downed plane. On this they threw ropes, parachutes, anything they could get their hands on. They poured high octane aviation gas on the bonfire.

As the plane approached, they ignited it. A column of thick black smoke shot up three hundred feet. The plane veered toward the smoke signal. It roared overhead, its wings dipping in happy salutes.

The Mariner circled and roared back again. From open windows it spewed parachute loads of food, clothes, blankets, medical supplies, a rifle, and ammunition.

Lieutenant Ball was at the controls. Coming in low, he saw that Captain Caldwell was wearing only lightweight khaki pants. He quickly stripped off his own flying suit and, making another pass over the group, tossed it out of the cockpit. Captain Caldwell said it was still warm from Ball's body heat when he slipped it on.

Ball's plane was running low on fuel so he had to return to the *Pine Island*. Another Mariner went out, commanded by Lieutenant Commander John D. Howell. By the time he returned, the six survivors were already on their way toward the open water, ten miles away, where the Mariner could land. Two of them were on sledges which were drawn by the others.

The elements almost defeated them again. When they were only a mile from the bay, a heavy fog settled in. The men could not see more than ten feet in front of them. Commander Howell, in the Mariner sitting on the water, realized what was happening. He started up his motors. Their roar was the beacon that guided the six to the water's edge.

A rubber life raft ferried the men to the plane. The fog began to lift. Commander Howell took off, dodging floating cakes of ice like a taxi driver darting in and out of traffic.

The plane landed and taxied up to the *Pine Island* three hours later. It was hoisted aboard and four men leaped to safety. The other two, Kearns and LeBlanc, on stretchers, were lowered carefully to the deck.

Six seamen lifted up LeBlanc's stretcher and as they did so, a gust of wind tore back the blanket covering him. The seamen gasped as they saw his swollen and scorched face.

"We were too late," one of the seamen said.

"No, fella," LeBlanc muttered. "You did a fine job. Thanks."

Before Operation Highjump ended, two more men were to die, making a total of five Americans lying buried in snowy graves in the Antarctic. But in spite of these tragic accidents, the operation was completed and termed another success in the struggle to learn more about the techniques of survival in the coldest regions on earth.

Nautilus
Ninety North

Every member of the crew, from the captain to the second cook, was worried. They were nervous. Some of them were frightened, but they joked about the situation to conceal their fear.

As one of the crewmen put it: "Here they give us a hundred-million-dollar home and the roof leaks!"

A leak ordinarily would be a very simple thing to fix. And ordinarily it would cause no great concern. But this was no ordinary situation. This was no ordinary leak. The "hundred-million-dollar home" was the atomic-powered submarine *Nautilus*. A leak in a submarine, topside, down below, anywhere, is a serious matter. The *Nautilus*

171

was sliding through the water, two hundred feet below the surface, on its way to the North Pole.

The leak had to be stopped.

The submarine captain, Commander William R. Anderson, his face grim, gave the order.

"Helmsman. Reverse course. We're going back to Seattle."

The *Nautilus* had been plagued with a series of difficulties, some large, some small, ever since the top secret order had been flashed from the Chief of Naval Operations in Washington to "execute Operation Sunshine."

"Operation Sunshine" was the code name for the long-planned, top-secret voyage of the *Nautilus* from Seattle, Washington, to Portland, England, by way of the North Pole. Never before had a submarine gone under the ice pack that covers the top of the world. Was there sufficient water between the bottom of the ice and the bottom of the ocean for a submarine to slip through? No one knew. What course should be set? No one had ever sailed those fearsome waters.

The *Nautilus* had tried it once before. She had gone under the ice to within striking distance of the Pole, where fingers of ice, extending downward forty and fifty feet, had to be dodged as if the sub were running an obstacle course. At times the *Nautilus* had to squeeze through water with its mast and bridge housing only a few feet from the ice above and its keel only a few feet from the ocean floor.

The first probe ended when the submarine reached a wall of ice barring their route. The door to the Pole was closed on their hopes.

After many delays, the order had come on June 8, 1958, to "execute Operation Sunshine," and the *Nautilus* was ice-pack bound.

And now she leaked. It was no wonder that Commander Anderson's broad shoulders drooped, his eyes were tired, his face lined with worry. But there was only one thing to do.

"Reverse course."

In Seattle, the ship's force went over the *Nautilus*, searching, probing the 100-million-dollar ship, trying to find the leak. They failed.

In desperation, Commander Anderson consulted with his engineering officer, Lieutenant Commander Paul Early, rated one of the best nuclear engineers in the business.

"Paul, what do you think of this idea?" Commander Anderson asked. "I want you to send your men around town in civilian clothes to various gasoline stations. I want each man to buy several cans of that stuff you pour into automobile radiators to stop leaks. What do they call it?—Stop Leak."

Early smiled. He didn't know whether his commanding officer was serious or just pulling his leg.

"I'm dead serious, Paul," Commander Anderson continued. "Nothing else has worked. Let's get about thirty gallons of the stuff. It comes in quart cans, so we'll need a heck of a lot of cans. But remember this—tell your men not, I repeat *not*, to disclose the fact that they're from the *Nautilus*. I guess you can imagine what people would think if they knew we had to fix up this multimillion-dollar baby with a can of Stop Leak."

"Aye, aye, Skipper."

"Operation Stop Leak" went into immediate execution. The leak was in the condenser system. This was the second leak to plague the *Nautilus*. On its earlier trip, a leak developed in the number one periscope. It had been badly packed, and when anyone used it a trickle of cold salt water ran down the user's back.

The periscope had been fixed, but the leak in the steam condenser system was a much more serious matter. The leak, which could be occurring in any one of ten thousand tubes and fittings, was emptying onto a critical piece of machinery. Until it could be stopped, the fate of the polar transit hung in the balance. Commander Anderson knew he could not expose his crew and his submarine to the danger of having a major piece of the propulsion machinery break down when the submarine was under the polar ice pack.

The idea of using Stop Leak was as wild as any tale ever spun by an old salt. But it worked. The leak was stopped. Cheers rattled against the ship's hull as the commander announced the success of "Operation Stop Leak."

Mooring lines were cast off. The *Nautilus* crept through the heavy traffic of Seattle Harbor. Her nose was pointed northward. Everyone in the ship was thinking the same thing: "This is it."

On the first of August, Commander Anderson gave the order to helmsman David Greenhill:

"Come left to north."

Dead ahead was the North Pole—1,094 miles away. Above, the Arctic was as bleak and cold as ever. In the *Nautilus* the temperature was a comfortable 72°; the food was delicious; the movies, entertaining.

The next day, the *Nautilus,* with its crew of 116 officers and men, was at cruising speed, running four hundred feet beneath the surface—her course 000 true north.

The tremendous submarine made a rapid run.

On August third, at ten hundred hours, the proud craft crossed Latitude 87° North. With every passing mile, the ship moved farther north than any other naval craft in history.

When the *Nautilus* was two hours south of the Pole, a wave of tense excitement washed through the ship. Every man was proud. Even those off duty gave up their "sack" time to be alert at the moment the *Nautilus* reached the Pole. They stood in tight groups, uttering the one word which they always used for the never-ending triumphs of the ship—"Fan-damn-tastic!" They'd make it! They felt sure. The *Nautilus* would hit Latitude 90° North, the exact geographical designation of the North Pole.

No bells would ring, no whistles would blow, when the *Nautilus* reached the Pole. There would be nothing to bump into. But the highly accurate, super-sensitive instruments on the ship would guide the submarine right to the Pole—she would hit it "on the nose."

By this time the submarine had been running under ice for sixty-two hours. The ice pack varied in thickness from eight to eighty feet.

When the *Nautilus* was one mile short of the Pole and closing in on it rapidly, Commander Anderson stepped to the ship's public-address system.

"All hands—this is the captain speaking. In a few moments the *Nautilus* will realize a goal long a dream of mankind—the attainment by ship of the North Geographic Pole. With continued Godspeed, in less than two days we will record an even more historic first: the completion of a rapid transpolar voyage from the Pacific to the Atlantic Ocean.

"The distance to the Pole is now precisely four tenths of a mile. As we approach, let us pause in silence dedicated with our thanks for the blessings that have been ours during this remarkable voyage—our prayers for lasting world peace, and in solemn tribute to those who have preceded us, whether in victory or defeat."

Silence followed the captain's words. The jukebox was shut off. The only noise was the steady pinging from the ship's sonars, the sensitive instruments which watched the bottom below, the ice above, and the dark waters dead ahead.

Commander Anderson looked at the distance indicator and started the countdown.

"Stand by. Ten . . . eight . . . six . . . four . . . three . . . two . . . one. MARK! August third, 1958, Time, twenty-three fifteen hours (eleven fifteen P.M. Eastern Daylight Saving Time). For the United States Navy, the North Pole!"

Cheers rang out. The cook brought in a huge cake.

Commander Anderson looked at Tom Curtis, a civilian technical representative.

"Did we hit it on the nose?"

"Captain," Curtis sang out, "as a matter of fact, you might say we pierced the Pole!"

Two days later the *Nautilus* surfaced in open water off Greenland. A short radio message went out to President Eisenhower that was to thrill the whole world. The simple sentence was:

"*Nautilus* ninety North!"

Up Through the Ice!

"Stand by to surface!"

The captain barked the crisp order. Tension in the submarine was thick—and so was the ice above.

"Aye, aye, sir!"

Commander James Calvert, skipper of the nuclear-powered submarine *Skate,* gripped the handles of the periscope until his knuckles were white. His mouth was dry. Beads of perspiration popped on his forehead.

The *Skate* lay directly beneath the North Pole.

"Speed?" the captain asked.

"One-half knot."

"Depth?"

"One-eighty."

The *Skate* was 180 feet beneath the ice which covered the top of the world.

"All back one-third."

Control levers were thrown. The submarine went into reverse.

A gentle shudder ran through the ship as her two eight-foot bronze propellers bit into the water, bringing the submarine to a stop.

"Speed zero."

"All stop," the captain ordered.

A chilled silence came over the ship as the vibration from the propellers ceased.

Commander Calvert felt the eyes of every man crowded into the control room burning into the back of his neck. He knew the question that was in every mind. Would he try it? Would he dare try to raise that submarine straight up, 180 feet, increasing its speed of ascent until it struck the bottom of the ice and smashed through?

Could it be done? Or would the heavy ice flatten the top of the sub? No one wanted to think of that possibility. One hundred and seven men refused to think of a finish in the dark arctic waters.

The answer came quickly. The captain was a man of action.

"Stand by to hit the ice!" He snapped the order, his voice strained.

"Bring her up!"

The submarine began her slow rise. She gathered speed. All aboard felt as if they were in an elevator, gaining speed as it shot upward.

"Heavy ice overhead! Thicker than twelve feet!" Officer Al Kelln at the ice detector shouted the warning.

"Flood her down!"

The *Skate's* upward movement came to a halt.

Commander Calvert snapped his orders as the *Skate* maneuvered for another try.

"Call out the depths as she comes up," Captain Calvert ordered Diving Officer Shaffer. "Bring her up!"

Once again the *Skate* rose toward the ice ceiling above her.

"One-forty," Shaffer called out.

"Up periscope!"

The periscope shot up like a snake preparing to strike.

"One-twenty." Shaffer continued his chant.

The *Skate* moved upward.

"One hundred!"

A moment passed. The top of the *Skate* was only twenty-five feet from the ice.

"Heavy ice! Heavy ice!" Kelln shouted from the ice detector.

"Flood her down—emergency!" Calvert cracked out the order.

A wave of air pressure popped ears as Shaffer opened the vent of the negative tank, sending tons of water pouring into the ship to bring her down. The sub swiftly dropped away from the dangerous ice cliffs above.

"Blow negative to the mark!" This order came from Diving Officer Shaffer. The *Skate* was dropping too swiftly. A roar of high-pressure air swept into the ship, forcing out the water.

Slowly the downward plunge of the *Skate* was checked. Finally, far deeper than the sub was intended to go, it became motionless.

The strain was apparent in every man's face. They had tried to crack upward through the ice and had failed. Was this to be the fate of the mission, for the second time?

The *Skate* had cruised these frigid waters seven months before in August, 1958. She had surfaced through the ice pack nine times and had demonstrated the feasibility of naval under-ice operations. Her first cruise had taken place during the arctic summer when air temperature seldom dropped below 32° Fahrenheit. In this comparative warmth, the thick polar ice breaks up in many places. Lakes and leads—narrow strips of open water—are formed. But even with these advantages, the *Skate* had been unable to surface at the Pole.

The *Nautilus* already had had the honor of being the first submarine to reach the Pole. For the crew of the *Skate*, the primary objective of this cruise was to surface at the Pole. This would be carrying out the sealed orders covering the operation for this cruise with a flourish. Those orders were burned into Commander Calvert's mind:

"Item one," the orders began. "Develop techniques for surfacing in pack ice areas. All other items are subordinate to this one.... The military usefulness of an ocean area is dependent on at least periodic access to its surface."

The Arctic Ocean is huge. It is five times as large as the Mediterranean Sea. It is nearly twice as large as the United States. Most importantly, it lies directly between the two heartlands of the world—the Eastern and Western Hemispheres. For military purposes, the Arctic Ocean is an area of destiny.

So the *Skate* was back. She had proved a missile-carrying submarine could be operational in the summer, but what about the winter? And, —a big *and*—would she be able to surface at the Pole?

It was March, 1959. Just as 3:00 A.M. is

usually the coldest hour of the night, March, the third month of the year, is the coldest month of the winter according to the meteorologists. At this time of the year, polar ice forms at the rate of six inches every twenty-four hours. The average thickness of the polar ice is ten feet, as against eight feet in the summer.

Could the *Skate* surface in the dead of winter? Could she surface precisely at the North Pole? She had been unable to do so on her summer cruise. The attempt now would be even more dangerous.

The *Skate* had been under the heavy winter ice for several days. She had surfaced, showing the practicability of winter operations. How many times she surfaced on this cruise and through what thicknesses of ice is top secret. But the driving desire of the skipper and the crew still was to surface at the Pole, to be the first ship to ride at the top of the world. The *Nautilus* had gone *under* the Pole—she had "pierced" it. But no ship in history had ever rested at exactly Latitude 90°

North, the geographic North Pole.

In searching for openings the *Skate* could shoot up through, the skilled crew had developed a new technique. The crew had expanded the use of the Fathometer, the ice detector. This delicate instrument bounces electronic signals off the ice above. Timing the signal's echo gives the distance from the top of the submarine to the bottom of the ice above. A second echo comes from the top of the ice. Comparing the two echoes gives the thickness of the ice.

When the *Skate* cruised under solid ice, the Fathometer gave a continual cross-section of the ice above. This pattern was drawn on a revolving roll of graph paper by a stylus pen, giving off a soft *swish, swish*. When the *Skate* slipped under open water, the stylus drew a straight, solid black line.

Eyes were constantly glued on the ice detector, ever watching for that straight black line. It did not appear very often during that second cruise. Whenever it did, of course, the *Skate* surfaced.

But open water came too infrequently for Commander Calvert's satisfaction.

This led to the development of a second and more dangerous technique for surfacing—crashing through the ice. The shell of the *Skate*, strong as it was, would never take a crash through ice ten feet thick. The search was for thinner ice. The thin ice permitted daylight to filter through. Thin ice is formed when a lead or polynya is recently frozen over. *Polynya* is a Russian word meaning a water opening in the ice. A *polynya* differs from a lead. A lead is a narrow crack between the ice floes. A *polynya* is an irregularly shaped, fairly round or rectangular body of water.

The newly frozen leads or *polynyas* were named "skylights" by Dr. Waldo K. Lyon, the civilian scientist on board. The thickness of the ice forming these skylights remains a top naval secret. Other nations would value this information highly.

Search for skylights was continuous. To locate them, Commander Calvert would raise the *Skate* to within one hundred feet or less from the bottom of the ice. The periscope would be "upped" and Commander Calvert would "walk it around," turning it in a complete circle, trying to spot a skylight. On March 17, 1959, the *Skate* was two hundred feet beneath the North Pole.

"Bring her up to one hundred," Commander Calvert ordered.

Slowly the submarine rose to the position ordered.

"Up periscope!"

The shiny steel cylinder hissed as it flew up in position.

Commander Calvert glued his eyes to the viewing glass. No skylight.

"Down periscope! Take her down to one-eighty."

Commander Calvert turned to the navigator.

"We'll crisscross this immediate area until we find a skylight."

At one-third ahead, about six knots, one hundred feet below the ice, the *Skate* spent hours going back and forth, up and down, beneath the Pole. No one had much hope. But Commander Calvert knew the ice above was shifting. At any time, the slow-moving ice might bring a skylight directly over the Pole.

Hours went by. The commander's determination was transferred to his crew.

Then he saw it—a faint glimmer of emerald green. Everyone knew a skylight had been found when they heard the skipper's barked order.

"All back one-third."

The *Skate* slid to a stop.

The moment had come.

The *Skate* drifted up to one hundred feet, Officer Shaffer chanting off each foot of ascent. This was a delicate, precise task. A submarine is not designed to rise straight up, or to sink straight down. Its upward and downward movements are controlled by diving planes, huge fins on the prow of the craft. These can only be effective when the ship is in motion.

There could be no motion here, either forward or backward. The *Skate* had to be raised by compressed air, forcing water out of her ballast tanks, and lowered by opening the negative vent and allowing sea water to rush in.

Twice the *Skate* rose upward. Twice the skipper had to call for flooding to prevent her from crashing into heavy ice.

Commander Calvert decided on a third try. He had the sub maneuvered until she lay just ahead of the floating skylight above. It was his

intention to have the *Skate* rise at the precise
second the skylight floated overhead. It was a
tricky, risky maneuver.

"Bring her up!"

The *Skate* began her climb. The steady whir
of the trimming pump—the mechanism which let
in the compressed air—signaled the rise.

Commander Calvert was at the periscope.
Nearer and nearer came the *Skate* to the ice
above. The emerald-green skylight became
clearer.

"Down periscope!" Commander Calvert could
not risk damaging the slender pole containing
the ship's eye. It would be the *Skate's* "sail," the
conning tower, which would strike the ice above.

"Stand by to hit the ice!"

The entire ship tensed.

The *Skate* struck the bottom of the ice. The
men aboard felt as if they were in a fast-rising
elevator brought to a sudden halt. With a frightening lurch, the *Skate* hit the ice—and cracked
an opening in it.

"Hold her there, Guy," Calvert shouted to Shaffer.

Shaffer shot more air into the ballast tanks.

"Up periscope!" The tube shot into open sky.

"Stand by to surface at the Pole!" Commander Calvert shouted exultantly.

"Aye, aye, sir. Ready to surface at the Pole."

The *Skate* began to crunch against the ice, which was heavier than Skipper Calvert had anticipated. Through the periscope, the commander could see the ice begin to buckle, crack, and split as the great bulk surged upward.

Shaffer continued to blow the main ballast; air poured into the tanks.

With a final pop, like a cork being released from the bottom of a tube, the length of the *Skate* cracked through the ice!

The goal had been achieved. The *Skate* sat exactly on top of the world, the first ship of any kind in history to do so.

From any position, ahead, astern, to port or starboard, the direction was due south!

City Under Ice

Take a hot shower in a cake of ice . . . sip a steaming cup of coffee and munch a crusty, warm doughnut under forty feet of snow. . . . Ideas for a fantastic movie? Not at all. These everyday bits of normal living occur daily in a real city under the ice. Above that city the temperature is 72 degrees below zero. Blizzards rage with winds at 110 miles an hour. But who cares when all the comforts of home are at hand?

The city is named Camp Century. It is a United States Army installation buried beneath the Greenland icecap. It is only three hundred miles south of the Arctic Circle, another thousand miles away from the North Pole.

One hundred men live in the city under the ice. They live in twenty-one tunnels. "Main Street," one of the tunnels, is paved and is eleven hundred feet long.

This city has just about everything: a laundry, a gymnasium, a garage, a library, a barber shop, a hospital fully equipped with an X-ray unit and an operating room.

What is this city doing 'way up in the frozen north? Why was it built?

Camp Century is the working model of the Army's newest sub-snow base. At present it is used solely as a research base. In years to come, the experiences gained there, the information gathered, can be of vital importance to America's military strength. Located near the top of the world, it overlooks the heartlands of the two great continents of the Northern Hemisphere. If a global war should ever come, the military value of such installations as Camp Century would be extremely important.

That cake of ice with the built-in shower is a

big one. The Greenland icecap spreads over 715,000 square miles, an area more than twice the size of the state of Texas. The icecap covers all of Greenland except for a narrow strip along the island's shorelines.

Until 1916 the United States had a legitimate claim to Northern Greenland because of exploraー tions and discoveries made by Peary and Greely. It gave up these claims to Denmark at that time in exchange for possession of the Virgin Islands, which were badly needed as refueling bases for the United States Navy.

Not until World War II did Greenland receive serious consideration for military operations. During the war, weather stations and emergency air fields were installed. With the development of the Intercontinental Ballistic Missile, Greenland became a significant area for military operations.

Camp Century came into being. It is located 138 miles east of our bustling air base at Thule, just north of Melville Bay. The Army Corps of Engineers had been conducting investigations into

arctic conditions for many years, as far back as
Operation Highjump in 1947, before work on
Camp Century was started in 1959, but building
this camp presented problems the Corps had never
been confronted with before.

Army researchers pored over the records left
by the great explorers—Nansen, Peary, Greely,
Amundsen, Stefanson, Wilkins, Ross—of all the
expeditions into the Far North. Each made some
contribution to the work now beginning.

From studying Eskimo survival techniques, the
idea of sub-surface tunnels, roadways, and struc-
tures came into being. Eskimos, during the winter,
go underground to live.

Once the decision was made to establish a sub-
surface camp, the big problem confronting the
engineers was how to reach the icecap. Along the
coastline of Greenland the icecap ends abruptly
in perpendicular cliffs from one hundred to 250
feet high. Only a narrow strip of ice-free land
remains between the cliffs and the waters of Baffin
Bay and the Arctic Ocean.

Those icy cliffs could be scaled. Construction materials could be raised to the plateau above. But there still remained another major problem. Extending back from the edge of the cliffs, the plateau is seamed by yawning crevasses, seventy-five to one hundred feet deep, and fifty feet wide. It would be impossible to bridge these shifting crevasses to make it safe to carry heavy equipment over them.

Experimental tunnels were bored into the base of the cliff, slanting upward to the plateau above. It was found that drilling these tunnels was not too expensive. They were bored far enough back to reach the crevasse-free area before coming to the surface of the plateau.

Once the crevasse-free plateau was reached, a thundering, powerful machine was brought into action. This is a machine developed by the Swiss. It is called a "Peter snow-miller." It mills ice-hard snow just as wheat is milled into flour. The snow-millers can cut a gash in the glacial ice and snow at the rate of three hundred to 350 feet an hour.

By going over the same gash again and again, the cut can be made as deep as desired.

The Peter snow-millers first dug a trench eleven hundred feet long—Camp Century's Main Street. They roared over their first cut again and again until the trench was twenty-eight feet deep and twenty-six feet wide. Corrugated iron arches were placed across this trench. When these were all in position, the snow-millers went back to work again. They sprayed milled, powdered snow over the arches. This snow froze quickly and became the roof of the tunnel.

Other tunnels were dug at right angles to Main Street—twelve of them. Into these tunnels were placed prefabricated buildings, flown into the camp by huge Army freight planes. Sanitation equipment was installed—also lighting, a kitchen, and a mess hall.

Power came from a nuclear reactor designed for the camp.

How to get water was a problem. It was solved by the Engineer Research and Development

Laboratories. They devised a steam drill. With it they bored a hole four feet in diameter and 165 feet straight down from the floor of the trench. There, the steam melted the pure ice into a wide well. Water is raised by a deep well pump. The men stationed at Camp Century have the purest water in the world.

The food these "ice worms" eat is a far shout and holler from that eaten by polar explorers of the past. No starvation diet of pemmican, seal blubber, and bear fat for these men.

For breakfast they may have a choice of large tumblers of juice, then eggs and bacon, hot cakes, hot biscuits, plenty of butter for their toast, jam, jelly, and, of course, coffee.

By mid-day they are starving again. Lunch is two double hamburgers, macaroni and cheese, po-tatoes—mashed, home-fried, and French-fried—creamed corn, salad, fresh fruit, pie, cake, milk, and—coffee.

Stuffed? Hardly. Dinner: steak, as much as they want, potatoes, hot gravy, stewed tomatoes, salad, hot biscuits, oranges, apples, lemonade or grape juice (cooled by glacial ice cubes), pie, cake—and coffee.

In the recreation hall there are pool and Ping-pong tables, books, cards, magazines, and radios. Movies are shown every night.

It may seem like an easy life but it's not. The men serve duty tours of six months. They are isolated and far away from their families. Winds howl. Temperatures rarely rise above fifty below zero in the winter. And they work hard. During the period of continuous daylight, they lose all sense of time. They work in shifts of eight hours but often continue for eighteen hours at a stretch with time out only for meals. They enjoy doing it, and there is little else to do but work.

The men selected to be stationed at Camp Century undergo long and exhaustive psychiatric examinations. They can have no hidden fears or phobias. The one hundred men, living so closely together, must have even, friendly temperaments.

They are also given very thorough physical

examinations. No one with any indication of high blood pressure is assigned to Camp Century. In the annual operations report of 1960, the medical officer writes:

The high altitude (seven thousand feet) requires troops to undergo a period of altitude acclimation. Numerous nosebleeds and one case of incessant bleeding indicate a necessity for screening personnel with a tendency toward high blood pressure. . . . The most serious medical consideration encountered was a rash of swollen, cracked lips. About fifty percent of the participating troops suffered from this. Temperatures and constant wind factors were considered the cause. The morale remained high throughout, and it was noted that when troops had been hard pushed and should have been ready to rest, they were eager to continue their activities.

The men at Camp Century have every comfort, every protection research and science can develop. But the frozen North remains an enemy difficult to master. It fights back with the same howling gales, the same below-zero temperatures that it hurled at the daring explorers of long ago.

One of the most vicious of nature's weapons is the "white-out." White-outs are weird. They come from hard, biting snow crystals which, like a thick fog, cut visibility from three miles to three feet. When they strike, all outdoor operations must stop. The men literally cannot see the tops of their own feet.

White-outs are a major problem. Exhaustive studies have been made to control them. To get rid of them, a technique very similar to seeding clouds to make rain has been developed. Dry ice and solid carbon dioxide are dispersed into the white-out by helicopters, anchored balloons, and rockets.

Supplies must be trucked, tractored, and sledged the 138 miles from Camp Tuto, the base supply camp for Thule and Camp Century. For the first thirty miles after leaving the tunnel which leads to the icecap, the danger of crevasses still threatens. Preceding a "swing"—a convoy of trucks—is an electronic crevasse-detector. This instrument is mounted on weasels—small tracked vehicles—and looks like the land mine detectors used in World War II.

The crevasse-detector teams plant dark blue flags every hundred yards to stake out a safe path for the swings. Red flags warn of crevasses near-by. After going beyond the thirty-mile danger point, the markers are placed every two hundred yards. To warn of a sharp turn coming up, orange flags are used.

There are two types of swings, heavy swings and light swings. Light swings are made up of two or more "pole-cats." Pole-cats are 145-horse-power, tracked vehicles. The lead pole-cat has a radio operator in constant communication with Tuto, Century, and the vehicles behind him. This is necessary in case of a white-out, during which the vehicles might become separated and lost. The trailing vehicles carry six passengers and bounce them along over the rough ice at a speed of eight miles an hour.

Heavy swings are bigger ice trains. Powerful caterpillar tractors pull these trains. The trains are made up of large sledges and house trailers on skis. They move across the wind-swept ice at three miles an hour. The house trailers are called "wanigans," a name borrowed from the woodsmen of the Northwest, where it means "a mobile cookhouse."

These wanigans have bunks for twenty-four men, latrines, electric lights, and a cafeteria. It takes five days to travel the 138 miles from Tuto to Century.

The command wanigan is equipped like the pilot house of an ocean liner. It has radio, navigational charts, direction-finders, and every sort of instrument for measuring winds, temperatures, visibility, and humidity. It also has a complete toolroom for on-the-trail repairs.

A command order is posted in every vehicle of every swing. It reads:

> In case of storm or white-out HALT YOUR VEHICLE IMMEDIATELY. Wait patiently.

Because of the severity of the weather and the fast-striking white-outs, no pole-cat or wanigan ever goes out alone. Neither do helicopters or other planes making the run between Tuto and Century. Storms in the Arctic can stop radio communication faster than a power failure. Any pole-cat, wanigan, or plane caught alone in one of these storms would have no chance of survival.

The swing technique was developed by Captain Charles P. Townsend, a veteran polar weather troubleshooter. Once Captain Townsend violated his own order to halt and wait patiently and he nearly lost his life.

A report came in that a heavy swing on the way to Century was crippled. Repair parts for a broken generator were urgently needed. The men in the heavy swing had no heat, no light, no regular radio communication. The distress report had been sent on a hand-cranked portable radio.

Captain Townsend quickly ordered a rescue party of two weasels to rush to the scene. His rescue party was less than two miles out of Tuto when a "Phase Three" storm struck. Phase Three means a storm with winds above fifty-five miles per hour. The storm brought with it a white-out.

Captain Townsend got out of his vehicle. He did not "wait patiently." He knew there was a weather hut nearby. He had to find it to shelter his rescue party. He plunged forward into the screaming gale that roared over the ice. Ice coated his face. One eye was frozen shut. The captain stumbled, rolled down a *sastruga*—a wind-built snow ridge—and crashed right into the hut.

He pounded with all his might on the steel door. The storm noises were so loud no one inside heard him. He knew he would have to get back to his weasel. Stumbling, staggering, he fought his way back to his tractor. A cup of hot coffee warmed him. He raised the weather shack on the radio. It was only one hundred yards away but completely invisible in the white-out.

The meteorologist sent a man out toward the tractor with fifty yards of telephone wire tied to his body. Captain Townsend started out with fifty yards of nylon rope. If they did not meet, they could make their respective ways back by reeling in their wire and rope. But fortune was with them. They met, and the rope and wire were tied together. The men in the rescue party followed the line to the warmth and protection of the weather shack.

An hour later the storm stopped as quickly as it had struck. The rescue party reached the crippled heavy swing. Five days later, the men in the swing were happy to reach the comfort of their city under ice.

The men at Camp Century live in dormitories, not the old-fashioned barracks of the regulation army camp. These dorms are twelve feet high, seventy-six feet long, and sixteen feet wide. Each has its own recreation room and five electrically heated smaller rooms. Each of these has two double-deck bunks, rugs, dressers, wall lockers, chairs, and an overhead light.

A strange thing about heating these cubicles is that the dormitory itself has to be cooled. The heat from the electrical units, if not controlled, would raise temperatures to a point where the ice-covered corrugated iron trench arches might collapse in the melting walls. To overcome this, engineers have drilled holes sixteen feet deep out to the surface above each dorm and have installed fans which suck in below-zero air to keep the walls and roof frozen. It is cold in the recreation room, but warm in the sleeping rooms.

Camp Century, the city under the ice, is a city of contradictions. It's hot; it's cold. It's comfortable; it's miserable. Night is turned into day, day turned into night. Time becomes meaningless as GI and scientist labor toward improving this nation's military strength in one of the farthest and certainly coldest outposts in the world.

Epilogue

The North and South Poles have been conquered by man on foot, in the air, and under the frozen sea. Still, man's probing into the desolate areas of the Arctic and Antarctic goes on. Knowledge learned through trials by all the pioneers from Peary to the crew of the submarine *Skate* has been utilized. The airplane and the submarine now bring the Poles within ready access. Each day, huge jetliners speed over the North Pole on routine flights, closing the time gap between continents. Submarines rendezvous at the North Pole, surface at it, and strengthen this nation's defense against enemy attack.

But man is still learning much from the snow

and ice-capped areas covering the top and bottom of the earth. Valuable weather data taken from these areas brings man closer to the solution of the mysteries of storms, hurricanes, and typhoons. Survival tests continue as scientists study man's ability to resist seemingly impossible living conditions. Geologists study rocks and minerals taken from the vast ice-covered acres of the Antarctic, seeking clues to the Earth's beginnings, searching for further supplies of essential ores.

Today's civilization owes much to the men who pioneered in exploring the polar regions. They wrote some of the most thrilling chapters in man's continuing drive into the unknown.

Whitman ADVENTURE and MYSTERY Books

Adventure Stories for GIRLS and BOYS...

New Stories About Your Television Favorites...

TIMBER TRAIL RIDERS
The Long Trail North
The Texas Tenderfoot
The Luck of Black Diamond

THE BOBBSEY TWINS
In the Country
Merry Days Indoors and Out
At the Seashore

DONNA PARKER
In Hollywood
At Cherrydale
Special Agent
On Her Own
A Spring to Remember
Mystery at Arawak

TROY NESBIT SERIES
The Forest Fire Mystery
The Jinx of Payrock Canyon
Sand Dune Pony

Dr. Kildare
Assigned to Trouble

Janet Lennon
And the Angels
Adventure at Two Rivers
Camp Calamity

Walt Disney's Annette
The Mystery at Smugglers' Cove
The Desert Inn Mystery
Sierra Summer
The Mystery at Moonstone Bay

The Lennon Sisters
Secret of Holiday Island

Leave It to Beaver

Ripcord

The Beverly Hillbillies

Lassie
The Mystery at Blackberry Bog

Lucy
The Madcap Mystery